INTERNATIONAL ORGANIZATIONS SERIES
Edited by Jon Woronoff

1. *European Community,* by Desmond Dinan. 1993
2. *International Monetary Fund,* by Norman K. Humphreys. 1993
3. *International Organizations in Sub-Saharan Africa,* by Mark W. DeLancey and Terry M. Mays. 1994
4. *European Organizations,* by Derek W. Urwin. 1994
5. *International Tribunals,* by Boleslaw Adam Boczek. 1994
6. *International Food Agencies: FAO, WFP, WFC, IFAD,* by Ross B. Talbot. 1994
7. *Refugee and Disaster Relief Organizations,* by Robert F. Gorman. 1994

HISTORICAL DICTIONARY OF THE INTERNATIONAL FOOD AGENCIES FAO, WFP, WFC, IFAD

by
ROSS B. TALBOT

International Organizations Series, No. 6

The Scarecrow Press, Inc.
Metuchen, N.J., & London
1994

British Library Cataloguing-in-Publication data available

Library of Congress Cataloging-in-Publication Data

Talbot, Ross B.
  Historical dictionary of the international food agencies : FAO,
WFP, WFC, IFAD / by Ross B. Talbot.
      p.   cm.—(International organizations series ; 6)
  Includes bibliographical references.
  ISBN 0-8108-2847-2 (acid-free paper)
    1. Food and Agriculture Organization of the United Nations—
History—Dictionaries.   2. World Food Programme—
History—Dictionaries.   3. International Fund for Agricultural
Development—History—Dictionaries.   4. World Food Coun-
cil—History—Dictionaries.   5. Food and Agriculture Organi-
zation of the United Nations—Bibliography.   6. World Food
Programme—Bibliography.   7. International Fund for Agricul-
tural Development—Bibliography.   8. World Food Council—
Bibliography.   9. Food supply—Dictionaries.   10. Food sup-
ply—Bibliography.   11. Food supply—Biography—Dictionaries.   I. Title.   II. Series : International organizations series
(Metuchen, N.J.) ; no. 6.
  HD9000.1.T34   1994
  363.8′83′03—dc20   94-2309

DEDICATED
to
Marva Coates (FAO Liaison Office, Washington, D.C.)
Patricia David (World Food Council, New York Office, UN)
Karen De Falco (WFP, Rome)
Vera Gathright & Leonora Grackin (IFAD Liaison Office,
Washington, D.C.)

CONTENTS

EDITOR'S FOREWORD

Within the ever expanding universe of international organizations are four apparently lesser stars. Best known by their acronyms—FAO, WFP, WFC, and IFAD—they do not shine with quite the brilliance of a World Bank or European Community. But they are no less significant in their own way. For the Food and Agriculture Organization, World Food Programme, World Food Council, and International Fund for Agricultural Development are occupied with one of the most fundamental challenges faced by mankind: how to feed a constantly growing population. They help in various ways—by improving agricultural techniques, by fighting pests and diseases, by creating better farmers, by tiding countries over in times of shortage, or by distributing food to the needy, all essential and worthy tasks.

With such important tasks, it is unfortunate that these organizations are not better known. In passing, it must be added that it is equally unfortunate that they are not more broadly and solidly supported by the international community and the general public. Certainly to fill the first gap, and hopefully also to lessen the second, this book makes a significant contribution. For it provides much of the basic information. This includes background on their creation, their goals and activities, their funding and personnel, the role played by key persons, what has been accomplished and what remains to be done. A chronology places events in the proper time frame and a list of acronyms is vital in detecting the players in international documentation. A bibliography points toward further sources of information.

Since there are four bodies, rather than just one, it was

somewhat harder to put together this volume. But the author, Ross Talbot, knows his way around. He has been studying the international food organizations since the late 1970s and has written numerous articles, book chapters, and a book *(The Four World Food Agencies)* on them. He has also lectured extensively, among other things as professor of political science at Iowa State University, where he is now professor emeritus.

Jon Woronoff
Series Editor

ACKNOWLEDGMENTS

Many persons have been of invaluable assistance in helping me put together this historical dictionary of the international food organizations in Rome, Italy. However, there have been two different groups of persons who have been of special assistance, and to whom I must, and am very pleased to, express my appreciation and gratitude.

(1) I have dedicated this book to staff persons who serve in the liaison offices of FAO, IFAD, and WFC in New York or Washington, D.C., and in WFP's Rome headquarters. Frankly, I don't know whether Ms. De Falco has supplied me with WFP documents since 1980, but to whomever has done so I'm indeed beholden. As for the others, we have met only via the telephone, but of this I'm certain: each has been wonderfully cooperative and instructive in supplying me with the necessary documents—from which I have "borrowed" often in preparing this dictionary. I'm greatly obligated to each of them.

(2) In that my typing and computer skills are almost naught, several persons have been of very considerable assistance to me in preparing this manuscript. I'm especially indebted to several splendid and skillful work-study students: Beth Krakau, Renee Ehrlich, Megan Scott and Jennifer Smyser, with a special kudo to Jack Whitmer's excellent secretary, Bev Christenson, who has assisted me far beyond any obligation she had to do so.

However, these acknowledgments should also include the usual and necessary exculpation: errors, wrong interpretations, and the like are my responsibility. Each of them is hereby pardoned.

ABBREVIATIONS AND ACRONYMS

ACC   Administrative Committee on Coordination
             (UN)

ADB   Asian Development Bank

AFC   Computer Services Centre (FAO)

AfDB   African Development Bank

AG   Agriculture Department (FAO)

AGE   Joint FAO/IAEA Division of Nuclear Tech-
             niques in Food and Agriculture

AGLINET   Worldwide network of Agricultural Libraries
             (FAO)

AGRINDEX   Index of worldwide produced publications on
             agriculture (FAO)

AGRIS   International Information System for the Ag-
             ricultural Sciences and Technology (FAO)

AID   (United States) Agency for International De-
             velopment

ASEAN   Association of Southeast Asian Nations

AT2010   *Agriculture: Toward 2010* (FAO study)

AUD	Office of Internal Audit, Inspection and Management Control (FAO)
CAP	Common Agricultural Policy (European Community)
CARIS	Current Agricultural Research Information System (FAO)
CCLM	Committee on Constitutional and Legal Matters (FAO)
CEC	Commission of the European Community
CFA	Committee on Food Policies and Programmes (WFP)
CFS	Committee on World Food Security (FAO)
CGFPI	Consultative Group on Food Production and Investment (abolished)
CGIAR	Consultative Group on International Agricultural Research
CIDA	Canadian International Development Agency
CIMMYT	International Centre for Maize and Wheat Improvement
COAG	Committee on Agriculture (FAO)
COFI	Committee on Fisheries (FAO)
COFO	Committee on Forestry (FAO)
CP	FAO/World Bank Cooperative Programme

DAC	Development Assistance Committee (OECD)
DANIDA	Danish International Development Agency
DD	Development Department (FAO)
DDC	Investment Centre (FAO)
D-G	Director-General (FAO)
EC	European Community
ECA	Economic Commission for Africa (UN)
ECDC	Economic Cooperation among Developing Countries
ECE	Economic Commission for Europe (UN)
ECLAC	Economic Commission for Latin America and the Caribbean (UN)
ECOSOC	Economic and Social Council (UN)
ECP	IFAD/NGO Extended Cooperation Programme (IFAD)
EEC	European Economic Community
ES	Economic and Social Policy Department (FAO)
ESCAP	Economic and Social Commission for Asia and the Pacific (UN)
ESCWA	Economic and Social Commission for Western Asia

FAC	Food Aid Convention (WFP)
FAO	Food and Agriculture Organization
FAOR	FAO Representative
FFHC/AD	Freedom from Hunger Campaign/Action for Development (FAO)
FI	Fisheries Department (FAO)
FINNIDA	Finnish Department of International Development Cooperation
FO	Forestry Department (FAO)
FP	Fertilizer Programme (FAO)
FSAS	Food Security Assistance Scheme (FAO)
GATT	General Agreement on Tariffs and Trade
GI	Department of General Affairs and Information (FAO)
GIEWS	Global Information and Early Warning System for Food and Agriculture (FAO)
HLIC	High-Level Intergovernmental Committee (IFAD)
IAA	Office for Inter-Agency Affairs (FAO)
IAEA	International Atomic Energy Agency
IBGPR	International Board for Plant Genetic Resources

IBRD	International Bank for Reconstruction and Development (World Bank)
ICN	International Conference on Nutrition
ICS	Interlinked Computer Storage and Processing System for Food and Agricultural
ICSC	International Civil Service Commission
IDA	International Development Association (branch of World Bank)
IDB	Inter-American Development Bank
IEFR	International Emergency Food Reserve (WFP)
IFAD	International Fund for Agricultural Development
IFPRI	International Food Policy Research Institute
IFS	International Fertilizer Supply Scheme (FAO)
IGG	Intergovernmental Groups (FAO)
IGO	Intergovernmental Organization
IIA	International Institute of Agriculture
ILO	International Labour Organisation
IMO	International Maritime Organization
INTERFAIS	International Food Aid Information System (WFP)

IPM	International Pest Management (FAO)
IPPC	International Plant Protection Convention
IRA	Immediate Response Account (WFP)
ISNAR	International Service for National Agricultural Research
ITSH	International Transport, Storage, and Handling (WFP)
IWA	International Wheat Agreement
IWC	International Wheat Council
JUI	Joint Inspection Unit (UN)
LDC	Least Developed Country
LNOR	Liaison Office for North America (FAO)
LUNO	Liaison Office with the United Nations (FAO)
NGO	Non-Governmental Organization
NIEO	New International Economic Order
OAS	Organization of American States
OAU	Organization of African Unity
ODG	Office of the Director-General (FAO)
OECD	Organization for Economic Cooperation and Development

OPEC	Organization of Petroleum Exporting Countries
OSRO	Office for Special Relief Operations (FAO)
PFL	Prevention of Food Losses (FAO)
PIC	Prior Informed Consent (FAO)
PRO	Protracted Refugee and Displaced Persons Projects (WFP)
PWB	Programme of Work and Budget (FAO)
RAFR	Regional Office for Africa (FAO)
RAPA	Regional Office for Asia and the Pacific (FAO)
REUR	Regional Office for Europe (FAO)
RLAC	Regional Office for Latin America and the Caribbean (FAO)
RNEA	Regional Office for the Near East (FAO)
SACRED	Scheme for Agricultural Credit Development (FAO)
SARD	Sustainable Agriculture and Rural Development
SCP	Subcommittee on Projects (WFP)
SIDP	Seed Improvement and Development Programme (FAO)

SOFA	*The State of Food and Agriculture* publication (FAO)
SPA	Special Programme for Sub-Saharan African Countries (IFAD)
SPM	Special Programming Mission (IFAD)
TAC	Technical Advisory Committee (CGIAR)
TCDC	Technical Cooperation among Developing Countries
TCP	Technical Cooperation Programme (FAO)
TFAP	Tropical Forestry Action Programme (FAO)
UNCED	United Nations Conference on Environment and Development
UNCLOS	United Nations Convention on the Law of the Sea
UNCTAD	United Nations Conference on Trade and Development
UNDP	United Nations Development Program
UNDRO	United States Disaster Relief Organization
UNEP	United Nations Environment Program
UNESCO	United Nations Educational, Scientific and Cultural Organization
UNFPA	United Nations Population Fund

UNHCR	United Nations High Commissioner for Refugees
UNICEF	United Nations Children's Fund
UNIDO	United Nations Industrial Development Organization
USDA	United States Department of Agriculture
WAICENT	World Agriculture Information Centre (FAO)
WB	World Bank
WCA	World Census of Agriculture
WCARRD	World Conference on Agrarian Reform and Rural Development
WFC	World Food Council
WFP	World Food Programme
WHO	World Health Organization
WID	Women-in-Development
WMO	World Meteorological Organization

CHRONOLOGY OF THE INTERNATIONAL FOOD AGENCIES

June 7, 1905	Establishment of International Institute of Agriculture (predecessor to FAO), Villa Borghese, Rome, Italy.
May 18–June 3, 1943	United Nations Conference on Food and Agriculture, Homestead Hotel, Hot Springs, Virginia.
October 16–November 1, 1945	Quebec Conference: First Session of FAO Conference, Quebec, Canada.
November 1, 1945	Sir John Boyd Orr was elected first Director-General of FAO.
November 4–11, 1947	First session of newly-created FAO Council was held in Washington, D.C.
November 11, 1951	Transfer of FAO from Washington, D.C., to Rome, Italy, was completed.
June 1954	FAO's Committee on Commodity Problems agreed to establish a Consultative Committee on Surplus Disposal, with its meetings to be held in Washington, D.C.
October 27, 1960	Initiation of FAO's Freedom from Hunger Campaign.

November 24 and December 19, 1961	Adoption, respectively, of concurrent resolutions by FAO Conference and UN General Assembly setting up World Food Programme on a three-year experimental basis.
December 1961	FAO/WHO Codex Alimentarius Commission was established, and is based in Rome. Implements Joint FAO/WHO Food Standards Programme.
June 4–18, 1963	First World Food Congress met in Washington, D.C.
April 2, 1964	Beginning of FAO/IBRD (World Bank) Cooperative Programme.
October 1964	Joint FAO/IAEA Division of Atomic Energy in Food and Agriculture was formed in Vienna, Austria.
December 6 and 20, 1965	Resolution adopted, respectively, by FAO Conference and UN General Assembly to continue World Food Programme on a quasi-permanent basis.
January 1, 1966	FOA's Fisheries Division elevated to departmental status.
June 20–July 2, 1966	UN/FAO World Conference on Land Reform held by FAO in conjunction with ILO, in Rome, Italy.
October 17–28, 1966	Presentation and discussion of FAO's first Indicative World Plan for Agriculture.

July 8, 1968   FAO/IBRD Cooperative Programme
                      was combined with other investment-
                      related activities into the FAO Invest-
                      ment Centre.

June 20, 1970   Second World Food Congress was
                      held in The Hague, Netherlands.

July 2–5, 1974   First meeting of Commission on
                      Fertilizers, in Rome.

November 5–16,   World Food Conference, held in
1974   Rome, Italy:

                      Resolution XIII—recommended the
                      establishment of an International
                      Fund for Agricultural Development
                      (IFAD)

                      Resolution XVI—recommended the
                      establishment of a Global Information
                      and Early Warning System by FAO.

                      Resolution XVII—endorsed FAO's
                      proposed International Undertaking on
                      World Food Security.

                      Resolution XVIII—recommended the
                      adoption of a ten million ton food aid
                      goal.

                      Resolution XXII—(1) called upon the
                      UNGA to establish a World Food
                      Council; (2) recommended that WFP's
                      Intergovernmental Committee be
                      reconstituted into a more powerful
                      Committee on Food Aid Policies and

Programmes (CFA); (3) recommended to FAO the establishment of a Committee on World Food Security as a Standing Committee of the FAO Council; (4) requested IBRD, FAO, and UNDP to organize a Consultative Group on Food Production and Investment in Developing Countries (CGFPI).

November 1974   International Undertaking on World Food Security was adopted by FAO Council.

June 23–27, 1975   First (annual) session of World Food Council was held in Rome, Italy.

September 1975   UN General Assembly resolution specified a 500,000 ton International Emergency Food Reserve, to be administered by WFP.

October 1975   FAO's Scheme for Agricultural Credit Development (SACRED) became operational.

June 13, 1976   International Fund for Agricultural Development (IFAD) was established as the thirteenth specialized agency of the United Nations, to be headquartered in Rome, Italy.

July 1976   Initiation of FAO's Technical Cooperation Programme (TCP)

December 20, 1976   Agreement establishing the International Fund for Agricultural Development (IFAD) was opened for signature by the Secretary-General of the United Nations.

June 20–27, 1977   World Food Council, at its third session, held in Manila, Philippines issued a communiqué which established a Programme of Action to Eradicate Hunger and Malnutrition.

November 1977   Initiation of FAO's Programme for the Prevention of Food Losses.

November 30, 1977   Agreement which established IFAD entered into force, after being ratified by countries pledging a total of $750 million to the fund.

December 13, 1977   IFAD's Governing Council held its first session and elected a President and an Executive Board. The Fund then became operational.

September 1978   Regional Food Plan for Africa developed by FAO, in cooperation with the Economic Commission for Africa.

July 12–20, 1979   World Conference on Agrarian Reform and Rural Development (WCARRD), sponsored by FAO, met in Rome, Italy.

October 16, 1981   FAO established World Food Day, to be celebrated throughout the world on October 16 each year, the anniversary of the founding of FAO.

November 7–25, 1981 — FAO Conference adopted the World Soil Charter.

FAO Conference approved the 1982–83 budget over the opposition of major donors, led by the United States.

June 1982 — First Replenishment of IFAD became effective with the deposit of instruments of contributions totaling over half of the respective OPEC and OECD pledges.

December 1982 — IFAD's Governing Council agreed that discussions on the Second Replenishment (IFAD-II) will begin in July 1983.

February 28, 1983 — Report by Elmer Staats, former U.S. Comptroller-General (The Staats Report), concluded that IFAD was well-managed but understaffed.

June 27, 1984 — FAO held in Rome, Italy, a World Conference on Fisheries Management and Development.

November 1984 — United Nations, in cooperation with World Food Council, commemorated the tenth anniversary of World Food Conference (November 15–16, 1974) in Rome, Italy.

March 1985 — FAO Commission on Plant Genetic Resources held its first session in Rome, Italy.

October 16, 1985	FAO celebrated its 40 years of service to humankind.
November 9–28, 1985	FAO Conference debated and approved World Food Security Compact—three member-states reserved their approval, including the United States.
	FAO Conference approved International Code of Conduct on the Distribution and Use of Pesticides. It is a voluntary, non-binding compact.
January 18–21, 1986	Meeting of IFAD's Governing Council resulted in an agreement to create a Second Replenishment (IFAD- II), at a level of $460 million—OECD ($276 million), OPEC ($184 million).
September 2–11, 1986	At 14th session of African Regional Conference, FAO presented its study—*African Agriculture: The Next 25 Years.*
January 18–21, 1986	The Governing Council (IFAD) amended IFAD's Articles of Agreement to extend the term of the President from three to four years.
January 26–29, 1988	IFAD celebrated its tenth year of operation.
May 23–26, 1988	World Food Council, meeting in Nicosia, Cyprus, received a report from its president entitled *The Cyprus*

Initiative Against Hunger in the World.

May 30–June 9, 1988	WFP's Committee on Food Aid agreed on a new method for deciding on projects. A Sub-Committee on Projects (SCP) was set up, for a three-year trial period.
May 22–25, 1989	The World Food Council, at its 15th session, in Cairo, Egypt, unanimously adopted a set of 11 conclusions and recommendations for the Alleviation of World Hunger, which came to be known as The Cairo Declaration.
June 1989	Agreement on a Third Replenishment for IFAD was reached at a reconvened meeting of its Governing Council, and was finalized in October. The agreed figure was $566.3 million, including a minor but important commitment by Category III members.
December 1990	International Wheat Council extended and expanded the provisions of the Food Aid Convention (FAC) of 1986 (a minimum annual level of donor contributions at 7.5 million tons of cereals) to June 30, 1993. FAC is implemented by WFP.
August 27, 1991	WFP and World Bank released their joint study titled *Food Aid in Africa: An Agenda for the 1990s.*

November 9–27, 1991	FAO Conference supported convening a fourth International Technical Conference on Plant Genetic Resources in late 1993 or early 1994.
January 1, 1992	WFP's revised General Regulations, which substantially increased its policy-making and decision-making authority, entered into force.
June 23–26, 1992	18th session of World Food Council, in Nairobi, Kenya.
December 5–11, 1992	International Conference on Nutrition (ICN), jointly sponsored by FAO and WHO, was held in Rome, Italy.
January 1993	16th session of IFAD's Governing Council was held in Rome, Italy.
May 31–June 4, 1993	It was announced that WFP has become the largest source of grant assistance to developing countries.
June 14–25, 1993	103rd session of FAO Council meets in Rome, Italy.

INTRODUCTION: FAO, WFP, WFC, IFAD

These acronyms signify the four world food organizations which are located and function today in Rome, Italy: Food and Agriculture Organization, World Food Programme (British spelling is used in Rome), World Food Council, and International Fund for Agricultural Development. For most of us they would be difficult to identify. If an inquiring pollster asked the respondent to state why we have four such international food agencies the results would likely be both unsurprising and disheartening. Nonetheless, these world food organizations are actively involved in assisting some 160 nation-states, especially the 130-plus developing nations, to achieve the following goals:

(1) raising the levels of nutrition and standards of living of the peoples under their respective jurisdictions;
(2) securing improvements in the efficiency of the production and distribution of all food and agricultural products;
(3) bettering the condition of rural populations;
(4) and thus contributing toward an expanding world economy and ensuring humanity's freedom from hunger.

Actually these goals are to be found, word for word, in the Preamble of the FAO's Constitution. However, the other three organizations would almost surely "sign on," if asked to do so.

The purpose of this historical dictionary is to enlighten the inquiring reader about the structure, functions, policies and

1

programs of these four organizations, along with sketches of their elected and appointed leaders. Politics, it has been said, is the study of "who gets what, when and how." Perhaps in this instance the word "does" would be a more operative verb than "gets," but the difference is not of major significance. If this study is successful in achieving its objective, all of us will have at least an overview of what these organizations do, and why, and may henceforth be more curious and inquiring about them. In words drawn from the 1974 World Food Conference, each of them is an important participant in the search for "the elimination of hunger and malnutrition . . . as well as the elimination of the causes that determine this situation." The realist, of course, would retort: "It can't be done." To this, the idealist will surely respond: "But we must try."

HISTORICAL SKETCH OF THE ROME FOOD AGENCIES

Because of the life, mission, and political acumen of David Lubin—a wealthy businessman/farmer from California—there did exist from 1908 to 1940 an International Institute of Agriculture (IIA). For historical reasons, which we need not investigate here, its home-base was also in Rome, Italy. By 1934, some 74 countries had become members of this institute. Among its several unique accomplishments, the IIA developed the first system for the worldwide collection of agricultural statistics and sponsored (for the first time) three international food-related conferences—locust control, wheat, and plant protection. But the rise of dictatorships, then World War II, caused the IIA's demise in 1940. However, its activities and contributions are well documented, and these can be found today in the David Lubin Library at the FAO in Rome. This is fitting, of course, because the IIA is the institutional, indeed the spiritual, forebearer of the Food and Agriculture Organization.

I. FAO: THE EARLY AND MIDDLE YEARS (1943–1974)

The original impetus toward a postwar world food organization apparently came from Frank McDougall, an Australian economist, a student of human nutrition, and a delegate to the League of Nations, who conceived the oft-quoted phrase, "the marriage of health and agriculture." In 1942, he wrote a memorandum on the subject of "a United Nations programme for freedom from want of food." (Freedom from Hunger was one of President Franklin Roosevelt's Four Freedoms.) Presumably Eleanor Roosevelt read and was impressed by the memorandum, and thereupon invited McDougall to the White House for dinner with the President and herself. Whether there is a cause and effect relationship here is still a mystery, but in early 1943, Roosevelt did call for a convening of a United Nations Conference on Food and Agriculture to be held in Hot Springs, Virginia, from 18 May to 3 June of that year.

Afterward an interim commission was set up, chaired by Lester Pearson, who was the Canadian ambassador to the United States, and over the next two years this group drafted what came to be the constitution of FAO. Thereupon, a signatory meeting was held in Quebec, Canada, on October 16, 1945. Some 34 nations were the original signatories, but by the time the first FAO Conference, which convened on October 17, 1945, had concluded ten more nations had joined.

Sir John Boyd Orr (later Lord Boyd Orr, who was already a prominent scientist-nutritionist, League of Nations activist, and member of the British House of Commons) was prevailed upon to become the first Director-General of this new international organization. After much doubt and uncertainty, Sir John undertook his new assignment and moved to Washington, D.C., to establish the first FAO headquarters.

By late 1945 and early 1946, it had become evident that all the basic ingredients for a major world food crisis were threatening. The UN General Assembly accorded that subject the first priority on its agenda, and Boyd Orr assumed that it was a propitious moment for him to make a major political move. With the General Assembly's complete approval in May 1946, Boyd Orr set up a special meeting on urgent food problems; the participants in turn asked him to prepare a set of proposals for dealing with immediate and long-term issues related to agriculture, food, and nutrition. The outcome was his proposal for a powerful international authority, to be named the World Food Board. In brief, this "was to be an international organization with power to buy, hold, and sell important agricultural commodities entering world trade, and to set maximum and minimum prices for these commodities in the international market."[1] It was a genuinely revolutionary proposal.

The World Food Board proposal was then submitted to the second FAO Conference, held in Copenhagen, Denmark, in September 1946. In turn, the conference set up a Preparatory Commission to study the proposal in detail. The commission's report recommended: (1) that the member-states retain their sovereign authority over agricultural and food-policy decisions; and (2) that a council should be established as a kind of ministerial body to the conference and the secretariat. (The Council, now enlarged from 18 to 49, presently functions in that role.) Thus, the World Food Board proposal was, in essence, defeated.

In 1949, after Norris Dodd had succeeded Lord Boyd Orr as FAO Director-General, the World Food Board concept was revised into a substantially subdued form to be called an International Commodity Clearing House. Again, a committee was designated to study the issue and submit a report; it subsequently proposed an International Commodity Clearing House to be set up to function as an action arm of FAO. The committee's report proposed a complex and

---

[1]Hambridge, Gove. *The Story of FAO.* New York: D. Van Nostrand and Co., 1955, p. 66. Also, FAO. *Millions Still Go Hungry.* Rome: FAO, 1957, pp. 35–36.

interesting procedure whereby this clearing house would dispose of grain surpluses, but let it suffice to say that the report was not accepted by the 1949 Conference. However, a Committee on Commodity Problems was established at that time, and in 1953 it proposed the setting up of an Emergency Food Reserve. This, too, was found unacceptable by the FAO governing body, but later (1954) a permanent Subcommittee on Surplus Disposal was set up. It continues to meet periodically in Washington, D.C., and reports each year to the Committee on Commodity Problems at its annual meeting in Rome. This subcommittee is almost toothless in terms of authority, but it does serve an informational function, largely by keeping food-surplus nations informed as to how the other nations are disposing of their food surpluses.

A major historical development during the first postwar decade was the crumbling of the European colonial empires in Asia, Africa, and (to a much lesser extent) South and Central America, and the rise into prominence and power of these new nations. Over time, they have generated enough unity and cohesion to form their own international interest group, the Group of 77, which now has some 128 members. On balance, however, it has not been a noticeably effective counter-balancing force to the rich nations.

This near explosion of new nation-states has its impact on FAO and all the other international organizations. There also were earlier manifestations that the postwar political power of the United States was gradually being challenged in terms of world food power. In 1949, after a sharply contested election, the FAO Conference decided to establish its permanent seat in Rome, not at its temporary headquarters in Washington, D.C.

In 1956, the first non-Westerner, B. R. Sen of India, was elected Director-General. (The second and third D-Gs were Americans.) Power had begun to shift slowly to the Third World. By 1964, with the formation of UNCTAD, the Group of 77 had formally organized and begun to function within

UN agencies as an international interest group representing the Third World countries. Within FAO this dramatic shift in the structure of power was also underway. In 1961, 22 new nations joined FAO, as did five more in 1963.

On the other hand, the bloc of Western Europe, North America, Japan, Australia and New Zealand (OECD) provides a very large percentage of the operating funds without which an international organization such as FAO would essentially be useless. In 1964, the Geneva Group (composed of all major UN contributors except the Soviet Union) was established as a kind of countervailing interest group to the Group of 77.

FAO's policy-making structure (See Charts and Tables, FAO 1) depicts a hierarchical policy-making process that culminates in the biennial conference to which every member-state is authorized to send a delegate, usually a delegation. Each member-state has one vote, although few votes are actually taken, which means that the developing nations have the preponderant numbers. Nevertheless, the Western countries, plus Japan, control the wealth. It is axiomatic in an international organization—where the doctrine of national sovereignty is still king—that the majority cannot command a minority to do what it chooses not to do.

As the process moves up the organizational hierarchy, it becomes increasingly political, although we should remember that cocoa, rice, wine, etc. also generate political controversy at times, especially so when world supply conditions are either too much or too little. Each member-state decides for itself whether it wishes to be a member of an Intergovernmental Group, of which there are 11. Their impact on subsequent policy developments is marginal, but they are not without influence.

The Programme and Finance Committees, both influential for obvious reasons, are limited in size and are carefully balanced between OECD and Group of 77 member-states. The FAO Council is not the ultimate authority, but its actual power is greater than that of the FAO Conference in that by the time major policy controversies have filtered up to the Conference level a compromise has usually been worked out in the Council. Worth noting is that 25 of the Council members are elected by the Conference from Africa, Asia and Latin America, while only eight are elected from the OECD nations.

The FAO Secretariat, especially the Director-General and the ranking officials, provide much of the organizational leadership. (See Charts and Tables, FAO 2.) Major policy proposals and program initiations are usually the product of the Secretariat, subject to their evaluation and ultimate decision by the member-states in the Conference.

The Secretariat is composed of nearly 7,000 persons, some 3,000 of them professionals, a Deputy Director-General (D-G), and 6 Assistant D-Gs. But the focus of this policy-making process centers around the authority and personality of the D-G. He is often autocratic in his relationship with the FAO bureaucracy, but is much more diplomatic in his dealings with the delegates of the member-states. The interests and the ideologies of the OECD members must be counterbalanced by those of the Group of 77, and within each there is considerable diversity, which creates conflicts of interests and ideologies. The position of Director-General calls for a consummate degree of political skill. The sociology of an international organization is more intricate and complicated than would ordinarily be true within a national bureaucracy.

II. FOUNDING AND IMPLEMENTING WFP

As already noted, Lord Boyd Orr, FAO's first Director-General, proposed in 1946 to establish a World Food Board, and among its several functions would have been the financing of surplus agricultural products for distribution to food-deficient countries. The proposal was much too revolutionary for its time, but the seeds of an idea were planted.

What caused this seed to grow was the vast accumulation of agricultural surpluses in the United States during the early 1950s Eisenhower administration (Ezra Taft Benson was Secretary of Agriculture).

To alleviate this food surplus problem, in 1954, the U.S. Congress passed the Agricultural Trade Development and Assistance Act (83–480), usually referred to as Public Law 480. Its initial purpose, in the legal phraseology of Public Law 480, was "to use the abundant agricultural productivity of the United States to combat hunger and malnutrition and to encourage economic development in the developing countries." This was to be done through making the surpluses available to food-deficit, low-income countries on grant or highly concessional terms.

Two studies on food aid were published by FAO during this period. Both were of seminal importance in understanding the possibilities and pitfalls of launching a multilateral food-aid program. The first study—*Disposal of Agricultural Surpluses*—written by Gerda Blau and published in 1954, demonstrated the possibilities of bridging the gap between the immediate desire to find additional uses for surpluses on the one hand, and the equally urgent need for long-term measures to foster growth and combat hunger in the developing nations on the other hand. The second, *Uses of Agricultural Surpluses to Finance Economic Development in Under-Developed Countries,* written by Mordecai Ezekiel and published in 1955, showed how food aid could be used to make it possible to increase the size of the development effort above what would otherwise be possible without incurring problems of inflation or balance-of-payment deficits. The theoretical and empirical research seemed to provide a solid foundation for the construction of a multilateral food-aid program. The issue had now become how to move from theory to practice.

In October 1960, the UN General Assembly passed a "Resolution for the Provision of Food Surpluses to Food-

Deficient Peoples through the United Nations system.'' Thereupon FAO Director-General Sen set up an expert group, chaired by H. W. Singer, to conceptualize a strategy whereby the UN objective could be implemented. In April 1961, their report was presented in Rome to a small inter-governmental advisory committee. One of the members of that committee was George McGovern, who had just been appointed by President John F. Kennedy as director of the newly created office of Food for Peace.

McGovern made a transatlantic phone call requesting clearance by the White House and the Departments of State and Agriculture to make an offer on behalf of the United States toward an initial world food program. His suggestion was a beginning effort of $100 million in farm commodities and exploring with Congress the possibility of $10 million in cash.

Within 24 hours, the White House authorized McGovern to offer such a proposal to Director-General Sen and the advisory committee, whereupon the foundation for WFP subsequently was laid of the food-surplus target of $100 million for the 1963–1965 triennium of which only $85 million was later pledged, $40 million of that amount being the U.S. contribution. But WFP had become operational, and in June 1962 its first Executive Director (A. H. Boerma of the Netherlands) was appointed and a new international bureaucracy began to function.

The major objective of the WFP program is to supply food for projects promoting social and economic development in recipient countries. A secondary responsibility is to allocate and deliver food surpluses to disaster areas—natural and man-made. Four types of regular projects are supported by the WFP:

(1) human resource development, such as child feeding and school lunch programs;
(2) infrastructure development, such as irrigation and

road projects, in which part of the workers' earnings are paid in food;

(3) production development projects, such as the supply of feed grain to support the livestock and poultry industries;

(4) resettlement programs to help displaced groups make a new start on land made available to them, until their first crops are harvested.

WFP is directed by a Committee on Food Aid Policies and Programmes (CFA). The terms of reference and membership of this governing body were broadened in line with a recommendation of the World Food Conference and an action subsequently taken by the FAO Conference and the UN General Assembly. The WFP governing body now consists of 42 member nations of the UN and FAO. Twenty-one members are elected by the Economic and Social Council (ECOSOC) of the UN, and 21 by the FAO Council. Members are elected for three-year terms and may be reelected.

The Executive Secretary of WFP is appointed for a four-year term by the UN Secretary General and the FAO Director-General. The program is administered by a joint UN-FAO unit headquarters in Rome. The staff in Rome carries on the day-to-day operations of the program, including the review of applications for aid, the arrangement of shipments from donor countries where commodities are stored until required, and appraisal of results. The program's representative in recipient countries originally was the resident representative of UNDP or the regional UN representative. Now WFP project advisers in the country are responsible to the UN officer. The WFP Executive Director submits progress reports to its Committee of Food Aid Policies and Programmes, which reports annually to the UN Economic and Social Council and to the FAO Council. They, in turn, report to the UN General Assembly and the FAO Conference, respectively.

III. THE WORLD FOOD CONFERENCE OF 1974

This conference, held in Rome, from November 5–16, 1974, was by far the most important world food conference that has ever been held. Was there really a world food crisis, immediate or on the near horizon? Students of the world food problem continue to argue that question, but the empirical evidence seems persuasive. In 1972, bad weather had caused world food production to fall slightly for the first time since the end of World War II. The increase in food production in 1973 was substantial, but not sufficient to prevent a further depletion of cereal stocks or to alleviate the continuing rise in world food prices. Also, there were major, sometimes severe, problems in the world economy—the energy crisis, inflation, worsening employment, monetary problems, fears of worldwide recession, and a general atmosphere of uncertainty and anxiety about the future. All of this significantly contributed to the calls for a world food conference.

Political factors were also evident. Third World countries were accelerating their demands for a new International Economic Order, and were being listened to in New York, Geneva, Paris, and Rome. U.S. Secretary of State Kissinger was desirous of taking action to mitigate this flurry of demands in order not to be controlled by and only responding to crisis events. For this, among other reasons, the UN General Assembly resolved in late 1973 that a world food conference should be held. Representatives from nearly all nation-states attended (including the Soviet bloc), as did representatives from most international agencies, 28 intergovernmental organizations, and 161 international and national nongovernmental organizations (NGOs). To quote from the provisional report of the Conference published subsequently by the UN Economic and Social Council: "Food was not only the major economic and social problem faced by the international community in the present difficult period of perplexity and change, but it was without question the most immediately important."[2]

Twenty-two resolutions were forthcoming; some, of course, were of more substance and immediacy than others. However, the point of particular emphasis to be stressed is: the resolutions of the Conference did, by and large, set the world food agenda for the following two decades. What must be emphasized is the impact the Conference and its decisions had on the activities, funding, structure, and stature of the Rome food agencies. Two of them—the World Food Council and IFAD—were creations of the Conference, so the politics of their origin will be stressed, first. The U.S. delegation (of 47 persons!) had been instructed by the Department of State: "No new Rome food agencies." But the political maneuvering at the Conference really made it a practical impossibility to adhere to that instruction.

A. World Food Council: Why and What?

The Conference delegates unanimously agreed to a "Declaration on the Eradication of Hunger and Malnutrition," in which it was proclaimed that "every man, woman, and child has the inalienable right to be free from hunger and malnutrition in order to develop fully and maintain their physical and mental facilities."[3]

Some 19 resolutions of the conference established a comprehensive strategy whereby these resolves could ostensibly be transformed into realities. Resolution XXII set forth

---

[2]UN Economic and Social Council. *World Food Conference,* E5587. New York: UN-ECOSOC, November 22, 1974, p. 13.
[3]Ibid., p. 57.

quite explicit institutional arrangements for follow-up action, and the first recommendation was a call for the UN General Assembly to establish a World Food Council with the following powers and responsibilities:

> "(c) the Council should review periodically major problems and policy issues affecting the world food situation, and the steps being proposed or taken to resolve them by Governments, by the United Nations system and its regional organizations, and should further recommend remedial action as appropriate. The scope of the Council's review should extend to all aspects of world food problems in order to adopt an integrated approach towards their solution;
>
> (d) the Council should establish its own programme of action for coordination of relevant United Nations bodies and agencies. While doing so, it should give special attention to the problems of the least developed countries and the countries most seriously affected;
>
> (e) the Council should maintain contacts with, receive reports from, give advice to, and make recommendations to United Nations bodies and agencies with regard to the formulation and follow-up of world food policies;
>
> (f) the Council should work in full co-operation with regional bodies to formulate and follow-up policies approved by the Council. Committees to be established by these regional bodies should be serviced by existing United Nations or FAO bodies in the region concerned."[4]

There was, of course, a political background to this creation. Some months prior to the opening of the World Food Conference, its secretariat had issued a comprehensive document, *The World Food Problem: Proposals for National and International Action,* and Chapter 20 proposed the establishment of a "perhaps to be called" World Food

---

[4]Ibid., p. 100.

Authority, which was "to implement or coordinate the implementation of appropriate recommendations and decision of the Conference."[5] Despite considerable advice to the contrary, Sayed Marei, the Conference's Secretary-General and a prominent Egyptian politician, apparently concurred with this proposal and proceeded to include it in his initial address to the Conference delegates.

On November 13, only four days before the Conference was to adjourn, a Contact Group set up by Committee Two surprised most of the delegates by coming forth with a proposal for a World Food Council, which would have "real authority." In essence, the council would "be able to issue directives to international bodies and governments."[6] Moreover, this new institution was to be set up and elected by the UN General Assembly. From that point on the "Storm Over Who Runs [the] Council," to quote a *PAN* (the Conference's nonofficial newspaper) headline, the Council became a major item on the Conference agenda, and the political maneuvers and negotiations became intense and somewhat complex. In essence, numerous members of the Group of 77 did not agree with the Contact Group's proposal, although 15 of the 22-member Contact Group were allied with the Group of 77. There was substantial opposition to having an international agency that would have "directive" authority, at least to the extent that it might be used to "direct" their own national governments.

Despite the instruction to the U.S. delegation that there was no need for new food institutions, Secretary of State Kissinger later became "an enthusiastic convert to the need for follow-up institutions." On the eve of the Conference, he personally instructed Ambassador Edwin Martin, his appointee to head the Office of Senior Advisor to the Secretary

---

[5]UN World Food Conference, *Summary of Principal Documentation . . . 2) The World Food Problem: Proposals for National and International Action.* Rome: FAO, 1974, p. 17 (working document).
[6]Ross B. Talbot. *The Four World Food Agencies in Rome.* Ames, Iowa: Iowa State University Press, 1990, p. 77.

of State, "to find an acceptable alternative to the Marei proposal."[7]

The "acceptable alternative" proved to be essentially what WFC now is. The UN General Assembly moved with unusual dispatch, and on December 17, 1974, it approved the establishment of a 36-nation WFC "at the ministerial or plenipotentiary level, reporting to the General Assembly through the Economic and Social Council and having the purposes, functions and mode of operations set forth in [World Food Conference] resolution XXII." Thus, by the end of 1974, a World Food Council had been established. As noted in the U.S. delegation's report: "While assigned a coordinating role, it [WFC] would have no authority beyond moral persuasion to force action on the part of governments or UN bodies.[8]

B. IFAD—Assisting "the poorest of the rural poor"

The creation of an International Fund for Agricultural Development was indirectly, but very significantly, related to the rise of OPEC as an effective negotiating instrument in the world political economy. Abetted by the Arab-Israeli war in October 1973, among other reasons, OPEC oil prices in the early 1970s increased in a near-exponential manner. However, rapidly spiraling oil prices were a severe burden to non-oil producing Third World countries, as well as those in the First World, and this did pose a delicate political problem for OPEC members, especially those from the Arab world. Politically speaking, the Arab OPEC countries had a dual strategy, relative to the creation of an IFAD: (1) to use their cartel power to force higher oil prices; and (2) to retain their

---

[7]Edwin M. Martin. *Conference Diplomacy, A Case Study: The World Food Conference, Rome, 1974.* Washington, D.C.: Georgetown University, p. 46.
[8]Earl L. Butz (U.S. Official Representative at the World Food Conference). *Official Report of the U.S. Delegation to the World Food Conference.* Washington, D.C.: USDA, November 1974, p. 29.

image and status as concerned and friendly Third World nations. This meant taking heavily from both the rich and the poor, and then redistributing some of these enormous profits back to the non-oil producing Third World Countries in the form of development assistance—some grants, mostly subsidized loans. It was within this framework of a unique politics of redistribution that IFAD was conceived.

The generally accepted explanation is that the OPEC countries proposed the fund (i.e., IFAD) in response to pressures put upon them to contribute more of their financial wealth to developing countries in general, and to their agricultural programs in particular, if only to offset the deleterious effects of higher cost energy on those programs. But the details of this "who did what, when, and how" in the formative days of IFAD are still not completely known. One prime mover was surely Sayed Ahmed Marei, who had been President of the People's Assembly of Egypt, and was later appointed in February 1974 to the influential position of Secretary-General of the World Food Conference. He has claimed that previous to that appointment the idea of an Arab-type Marshall Plan had been "revolving in his mind," and that the preparations previous to the conference had offered him "an opportunity to launch the idea for an International Fund for Agricultural Development." In any case, the Conference's secretariat proposed setting up an "Agricultural Development Fund, to provide grants, soft loans, and commercial loans for increasing food production in developing countries," although this was to be done within the much more elaborate and extensive framework of a World Food Authority. Predictably that proposal proved to be wholly unacceptable to the delegates at the subsequent conference.

Another plausible account has been put forth by Abdelmuhsin M. Al-Sudeary, who in 1974 was the Saudi Arabian ambassador to the Food and Agriculture Organization; he subsequently became the first President of IFAD. His version of the origins of IFAD follows:

> "I thought . . . that we should try to convince the govern-
> ments of my country and the other OPEC countries to
> concentrate on a single world fund to help in all these areas.
> So we sent a messenger with a hand written letter to King
> Faisal. In less than 24 hours he replied that Saudi Arabia
> would back it. Soon Iran and Venezuela had agreed, then the
> rest of OPEC. And by the end of the World Food Confer-
> ence, many of the developed and developing countries were
> with us."[9]

Although the behind-the-scenes activities of the OPEC
members are still obscure, we do know that a considerable
number of extended and controversial negotiations took
place. Indeed, it appeared until almost halfway through the
conference that no IFAD-type resolution would be forthcoming, but on November 14 such a proposal was announced. According to *PAN*—the populistic, unofficial,
irreverent, but widely read, conference newspaper—"within
two hours . . . the conference mood changed from gloom to
something approaching good cheer."

It is evident that the U.S. government had no particular
enthusiasm for the IFAD proposal. Its official position was
no new institutions, not much in new contributions. Edwin
Martin later contended, in his memoir of the Conference,
that the U.S. had never been negative with respect to the
creation of a fund to finance investment in food production
in developing countries on concessional terms. However,
Ambassador Martin confirmed that Washington's approval
for the creation of this new institution took some considerable convincing on his part, via cable; indeed, he observed
that "initially assurances were given to the conference
delegates that the U.S. had no present intention of contributing to the Fund, and would continue directing its substantial
multilateral contributions through existing institutions."

---

[9]For the source of this and other quotes concerning the establishment of the
IFAD, see: Talbot, *The World Food Agencies in Rome,* chapter 5.

Albeit, when Resolution XIII (the IFAD resolution) came to a vote on the conference floor there was only one dissenting vote—that of the Federal Republic of Germany (West Germany) on the grounds of its opposition to "new institutions," and not because of "new funds." But the first two provisions of the resolution boded ill for those who anticipated harmony and cooperation between the member-states of OECD and OPEC.

> "The World Food Conference, . . . resolves that:
>
> 1. An International Fund for Agricultural Development should be established immediately to finance agricultural development projects primarily for food production in the developing countries;
>
> 2. All developed countries and all those developing countries that are in a position to contribute to this fund should do so on a voluntary basis; . . . "

The subsequent negotiations did not result immediately in the establishment of a fund. That difficulty was implicit in the compromise which stated that the contributions would be made on a "voluntary basis." The Conference delegates, primarily from the rich nation-states, became involved in complex negotiations, wherein they were striving to protect and, hopefully, foster their various and different national interests. Nevertheless, the complicated process of creating a new international political institution had begun.

The World Food Conference's Resolution XIII stipulated that IFAD "should be established immediately to finance agricultural development projects primarily for food production in the developing countries." Even so, the "immediately" was stretched over a three-year period. On December 17, 1974, the UN General Assembly endorsed all the Conference's resolutions, but the first meeting of IFAD's governing council did not take place until December 13, 1977.[10]

Resolution XIII specified the setting up of a Governing Board (later to be renamed the Governing Council), with an "equitable distribution or representation," between the "contributing developed countries" (meaning OECD members), the "contributing developing countries" (meaning OPEC members), and "potential recipient states" (meaning the Group of 77). There also was to be "regional balance" among those receiving funds from IFAD (meaning that all developing countries should be recipients, not just the poorest.) The main obstacle centered around the questions, Who pays? Who receives? and, in particular, the implementation of the first clause. The resolution stated that contributors to the fund "should do so on a voluntary basis," a provision adamantly insisted on by the OECD member-states.

The $1 billion goal continued to be the principal obstacle. The United States, in particular, contended that there must be a "rough parity" (meaning 58–42 percent) between the OECD and OPEC contributions; OPEC interpreted this to mean $600 million from OECD, $400 million from OPEC. Pledges increased to $930 million; then John Hannah (the first Executive Director of the new World Food Council) did more traveling and persuading, but announced the new total was only $965 million. Saudi Arabia initiated the necessary compromise formula ($15.5 million more from OPEC, $19 million in additional pledges by OECD members). The total finally pledged was $1,011,776,023, with $9 million in convertible currency to be contributed by the recipient developing nations. This meant a formula of approximately 58% from OECD members, 42% from OPEC members.

---

[10]For more details and analysis, see: Ross B. Talbot, "The International Fund for Agricultural Development," *Political Science Quarterly,* vol. 95, no. 2 (1980), pp. 261–277.

(Other Third World countries pledged later.) IFAD was ready to go to work. The first session of the Governing Council met in Rome from December 13–16, 1977, and by that time 114 nation-states had joined this specialized agency.

C. FAO at the World Conference

By the time the World Food Conference was held FAO had been in operation for nearly 30 years. Its accomplishments were numerous, but much of the criticism concerning the world food crisis of the early 1970s was laid at its door. This was unfair. Nevertheless, in international politics (as in national politics) perceptions often constitute reality. FAO was believed to be: too bureaucratic—too unimaginative—increasingly inefficient, among other criticisms. The official report of the World Food Conference does attempt to exonerate FAO as a principal cause of the 1970s world food crisis. Quite correctly, it argues that FAO had foreseen the coming crisis, and had prescribed several programs and strategies for meeting that crisis. But political support, and notably but not exclusively funding, were not forthcoming. Nevertheless, the stigma was perceived to be real, and still exists, to a lesser extent, today.

Needless to say, perhaps, FAO opposed the creation of the World Food Council. Its existence was an obvious institutional insult, at least as seen by FAO. However, FAO's leadership was more accepting of IFAD. Its functions and programs, once implemented, would and did call for assistance from FAO regarding their implementation.

FAO's International Undertaking on World Food Security was endorsed by the World Food Conference. But it—and subsequent world food security proposals of FAO—have proven to be more rhetoric than substance, due to the refusal of the major wheat-producing countries to be bound by mandatory commitments.

However, a Conference resolution did "recommend" that the FAO should "establish a Committee on World Food Security as a standing committee of the FAO Council." This was done in 1975. The Committee is open to membership by any member-state, and most do participate in the two sessions which are held each biennium. The activities of the Committee keep this important issue alive and on the international agenda.

Also, Conference Resolution XVI mandated that a Global Information and Early Warning System on Food and Agriculture should be established, and that FAO would be "the most appropriate organization to operate and supervise the system." FAO has endeavored to give vigorous leadership to the implementation of that resolution. Satellites have been used for detecting crisis problems; several computerized programs are in operation for the quick dissemination of research data and findings; printed publications (such as the monthly *Food Outlook*) are widely disseminated.

Finally, Resolution III (Fertilizers) gave its endorsement to the establishment in 1973 of FAO's Commission on Fertilizers and its International Fertilizer Supply Scheme. For a few years subsequently, this commission and its program were energetically implemented and of value in the funding of fertilizer distribution programs to developing countries, although in recent years the funding (voluntary, by OECD countries) has declined dramatically.

D. WFP at the World Food Conference

Conference Resolution XVIII (An Improved Policy for Food Aid) directly and importantly concerned the World Food Programme. And the so-called "follow-up action" resolution (XXII) also gave some further strength to the prescribed reorganization of WFP. Its Intergovernmental Committee was to be reconstituted (enlarged—30 member countries, evenly divided between the rich and poor nations), and renamed the Committee on Food Aid Policies and Programmes (usually referred to as CFA). In turn, CFA was assigned "the task of formulating proposals for effective coordination of multilateral, bilateral and non-governmental food aid programmes and of coordinating emergency food aid." In brief, CFA had to legitimize the proposals for development projects and food relief programs submitted to it by the Executive Director.

In order to implement the concept of forward planning for food aid, Resolution XVII also "recommended" that the donor (rich, industrial) countries "make all efforts" to provide "at least 10 million tons of grains" for food aid—both bilateral and WFP food aid. In other words, the 10-million ton goal was actually a floor figure; hopefully the allocations would be higher, and in some recent years they have been.

Finally, that resolution gave positive support to the FAO's proposal of earmarking food stocks for emergency purposes. This provision was part of FAO's proposed International Undertaking on World Food Security. The "recommenda-tion" was significant to WFP in that "part of the proposed emergency stocks" were to be allocated to WFP for its utilization, although this recommendation later came to naught.

In summary, the 1974 World Food Conference was engaged in building an international agenda of future world food policies and, more concretely, in the creation and mandating of two new institutions (WFC, IFAD), and the remandating of the two already in operation (FAO, WFP). The rather utopian expectation was that these new and reformed institutions would provide some of the necessary leadership to transform the Conference resolutions into policies and programs, international and national, which would prove to be operational and effective. Again, how-ever, it must be remembered that international conference resolutions, as they pertain to member-states, only employ verbs like "recommend," "urge," "express," "vote," and "recall." The final decision as to what will actually happen remains with the (sovereign) member-states, rich or poor.

IV. POST-WORLD FOOD CONFERENCE DEVELOPMENTS

The 22 resolutions agreed to at the World Food Conference set the agenda for world food policy probably to the end of the century. Very briefly, the underlying and really quite specific objective of those resolutions was to try to persuade the industrial nations to support, financially and policy-wise, the agricultural development of Third World countries, and in turn for those new nations to generate sufficient internal political will to "put their own houses in order." In that very important endeavor the four world food agencies in Rome were expected to play a useful, secondary role. Policymaking of major stature was still to be decided by the main agricultural powers—United States, European Community (now European Union), Canada, Australia, a few Latin American countries, with Japan as a rather quiet but increasingly influential actor.

A. *World Food Council*

As noted previously, the World Food Council was the creation of the World Food Conference. Resolution XXII called upon the UN General Assembly to establish the World Food Council and to charge it with the responsibility of being the "co-ordinating mechanism . . . for the successful coordination and follow-up of [food] policies" of all types, national and international. However, the financial and political resources of the Council have never been such that it could more than meagerly fulfill its mandate. In some respects, the creation of the World Food Council was a direct, perhaps unintended, insult to the Food and Agriculture Organization. Unfairly, FAO had become the scapegoat for the world food crisis of the early 1970s. This is not to argue that the World Food Council has not been of some usefulness; it has sought, with marginal successes, to keep the generic "world food problem" on the international agenda. But it soon became evident that the Council had to struggle vigorously just to prevent itself from being abolished, absorbed, or both. It would be fair to contend that a World Food Council could become a constructive instrument in world food policy developments, but not under present conditions.

B. International Fund for Agricultural Development

The second institutional creation of the World Food Conference was the International Fund for Agricultural Development. Resolution XIII treats the IFAD exclusively, and specifies that it should be established immediately to finance agricultural development projects primarily for food production in the developing countries. One would have to conclude that IFAD has been a remarkably successful international organization, within the severe limitations in which it has had to function.

On the positive side, IFAD leadership has won the ideological battle. This organization was created to give assistance to "the poorest of the rural poor," and this goal it has pursued with vigor and imagination. In terms of symbolic politics, IFAD has been a major triumph. And policy–wise, IFAD has been able to create the impression, with considerable media support, that there is substance and content, as well as imagination and ingenuity in its programs and projects. That is, it stands at the cutting edge in its endeavors to alleviate poverty in the rural areas of the developing nations.

On the obverse side, IFAD was the creature of a power play by the OPEC countries, especially the Arab members, a major effort on their part to defend themselves against charges of greed and avarice which, without presumed intent, did serious harm to economic, social, and political developments in Third World countries. OPEC strategy, relative to matters concerning world food politics, was to challenge the OECD countries to match its "generosity" in providing the funds which would make it possible for IFAD to succeed in the fulfillment of its objective—at least that possibility was viewed to exist by its true believers. There is a long story here, but a brief account would be: OPEC's early successes in its accumulation of immense wealth have withered somewhat over the years, with the Iran-Iraq War and later the Gulf War as the major causal factors, among several others. Succinctly, IFAD has accomplished much, with less and less financial support from OPEC members and only begrudging assistance from OECD countries. Moreover, OECD members—led by the opposition of the United States—have with intent and success prevented IFAD from becoming more than a minor, ancillary bureaucracy.

At this moment (fall 1993) IFAD is extensively involved in negotiations which will hopefully lead to its fourth "replenishment." Those negotiations will likely be viewed as a success if the major contributors—now heavily OECD members—pledge contributions totaling $600 million, for a multiple year period.

C. World Food Programme

WFP has more political support, both from industrial and developing countries, than the other world food agencies. The basic reason underlying this situation is that WFP effectively uses the food production surpluses (surplus, that is, in terms of an effective demand worldwide for the food) to assist the developing nations to improve their economic condition and to alleviate the very serious problem of feeding millions of refugees. Indeed, this food-for-development strategy was the primary basis for creating a WFP institution in the early 1960s. Very roughly, of some ten million tons of food aid contributed annually in recent years by member countries (meaning primarily the United States, European Community and its member states, Canada, Australia, and the Scandinavian countries) about 20 percent is designated for use by WFP. In turn, most of this food is used by WFP to fund development projects of various types–e.g., agricultural production, rural infrastructure, settlement project food reserves, school and vulnerable group feeding—and increasingly, in recent years, to feed the millions of refugees in Africa and Asia.

Also, and to WFP's advantage, at least as viewed by its bureaucracy, is that after several years of feuding with FAO it now has been granted a considerable amount of policy and administrative autonomy. That is, some of the WFP policy decisions and administrative controls had to be approved (agreed to) by FAO officials. This festering condition has now been resolved, quite largely in WFP's favor.

On the adverse, or at least critical side of the evaluation ledger, WFP does have its problems. First, its funding comes primarily from voluntary pledges of member countries. The pledging target for 1994–95 is $1.5 billion (hopefully, one-third, in aggregate, in hard currencies) and that target will almost surely not be met. (Since 1978, the targets have been attained in percentages in the 80–90 percent range). Actually, that is probably as high a percentage as could reasonably be expected. These are voluntary pledges, and it is almost axiomatic that when the OECD countries are in a supply/demand situation which inflates the price of food in the home country it will cause a decrease in food contributed to WFP. Ergo, WFP is a hostage to the food situation in the rich nations.

Secondly, WFP is also the principal food contributor to disaster areas—Somalia, Cambodia, Afghanistan, among others. Indeed, in 1991 half of the food allocations made by WFP were to provide disaster relief—natural and man-made disasters—to these countries. Some 20 million people, including 14 million refugees and displaced persons, received WFP food relief in 1991. Of course, this was a humanitarian necessity, and politically it did give WFP some positive identification and publicity worldwide, but WFP's principal purpose and strategy is to use its resources as an economic development tool to assist poor countries. Therefore, the more food allocated to disaster relief, the less is available for development purposes.

So WFP's future is certainly not precarious, but nevertheless it is confronted with a number of serious challenges. Ironically, perhaps, weather worldwide is a most important exogenous control. But the probabilities seem to be in WFP's favor.

D. Food and Agriculture Organization

By almost any criteria one would choose to use, except that perhaps of public opinion, FAO is the premier world food institution—goals, funds, experience, expertise, number of personnel, etc. However, next to the World Food Council (a rank above WFC, by my estimate) FAO has the most serious critics. The cause for this organizational jeopardy had been referred to earlier—too bureaucratic, too inefficient, too elitist, too ineffective. In my judgment, many of these criticisms tend to be rationalizations (self-protection by OECD countries to cover their inadequate support of FAO), or superficial evaluations. But it is accurate, I believe, to claim that the criticisms do continue to be heard and believed.

FAO's authority has been gradually chipped away ever since the 1974 World Food Conference. FAO's Director-General and others in leadership positions have endeavored to check this power-bleeding, and to re-establish FAO's reputation and prestige. They have constantly tried to be innovators or promoters of cutting-edge issues: agrarian reform, rural development, improved nutrition, role of rural women, sustainable development, environmental improvements, among others. And they have surely had some success. But the main difficulty is that even when the member-states agree to the importance, indeed the vital need, of acting on these issues, they do not grant much additional authority and even less in new funding.

Perhaps I view this too much from a Middle America perspective, but FAO's principal weakness and danger at the moment is not that its critics are presently so damaging to its future, but more dangerously, that it is increasingly viewed as a minor actor in the field of world food policy.[11] At least it can be well-documented that FAO has been going through, and is still in, a very difficult financial condition. The figures change from month to month, but in 1991 73 member-states were in arrears to FAO, relative to the legal assessments they were obligated to fulfill, which means that almost half were in arrears; as of November 5, 1991, contributions in arrears totaled over $138 million. The United States was the major laggard, by far; its arrears on that date for 1990 and prior assessments was just over $116 million. This U.S. indebtedness has been lessened somewhat in recent months, but FAO's perplexing political problem continues to be evident—its perception as a flawed, marginal, low priority institution.

Whatever one's philosophy of history, it would seem that there would be an agreement on this proposition: what is will change. One can draw scenarios which show all these Rome world food agencies in more powerful and prestigious roles. Crisis is a powerful motivator of action. But the most likely scenario for these agencies, in my opinion, is one of holding the status quo. Perhaps, some incremental improvement in financial and political support for WFP and IFAD, less

---

[11]For a more detailed discussion, see Ross B. Talbot and H. Wayne Mayer, "Who Governs the Rome Food Agencies?," *Food Policy,* Vol. 12, No. 4, pp. 349–64.

financial harm to FAO but little more authority, and possibly the dissolution of the World Food Council. Hopefully, this will prove to be a flawed and too pessimistic prediction![12]

On the optimistic side of the future-ledger, new institutional and policy developments were evident in late 1993. FAO's Director-General (Saoma) has decided not to stand for reelection, so the Conference elected a new Director-General in November 1993. (I'm assuming that new leadership means a renewed dynamism). The UN General Assembly is considering a draft resolution, sponsored by Canada, Japan, and the United States, which presumably would restructure and revitalize the World Food Council. Actually, in my opinion, it would even further weaken that organization, and it seems likely that the developing nations will hold that viewpoint and not permit the resolution to pass. At any rate, the sponsoring countries claim that their proposal, if adopted by the General Assembly, "will greatly improve the utilization of resources for important and growing food and hunger problems . . . ."

WFP is in the midst of a political campaign to convince the industrial countries that allocations of food aid must be considerably increased (up to 30 million tons is being mentioned for the 1990s and on into the 21st century). And IFAD continues to display its effervescent optimism that, properly funded, it has the knowhow and the skill to assist economically poor countries in alleviating their formidable conditions of rural poverty.

---

[12]In recent months the offices of the World Food Council in Rome were vacated and its responsibilities were moved to the United Nations in New York City. There the functions of the WFC have apparently been transferred to the UN's new Department of Sustainable Development. Legally, the WFC continues to exist; most, if not all, of the Third World countries will not agree to its abolition, and they have a large majority of the votes in the UN General Assembly. However, as an international agency the World Food Council has been mothballed—waiting, one might speculate, for the next major world food crisis.

THE DICTIONARY

A. FOOD AND AGRICULTURE ORGANIZATION (FAO)

-A-

No entries

-B-

BOERMA, ADDEKE HENDRICK (A.H.) (1912-1992). Boerma was born in 1912 and educated in the Netherlands. After serving in the Netherlands Government Service, prior to, during, and after World War II, Boerma accepted a position in FAO, and by 1960 he had risen to the rank of Assistant D-G. Then in 1962, he was chosen by the United Nations and FAO to become the first Executive Director of the newly established World Food Programme. Elected in late 1967 to the position of FAO Director-General (q.v.), he served in that position until the end of 1975. Boerma's reputation as a D-G has not weathered well over the years. He was a consensus politician during a time in which there was growing disagreement between the Western industrial nations and the many, new developing nations. His role at the World Food Congress (q.v.) in 1970 was one of unsteady leadership in a time of considerable turmoil, and he was blamed (probably quite unfairly) for not showing proper leadership abilities in the early 1970s when the world was involved in a food crisis of historic proportions. This predicament resulted in the calling by the United Nations of a World Food Conference (q.v.) in 1974, and the creation of new world food organizations which were not responsible to, or favored by FAO.

-C-

CARDON, PHILIP V. (1889-1965). A U.S. citizen, born in Logan, Utah, he received a B.Sc. degree from Utah State, and then a Master's degree in agricultural economics from the University of California. Cardon was a researcher, an academic, a one-time newspaper editor, then Director of the Utah State Experiment Station, from which position he moved to the Department of Agriculture (USDA) where he became Administrator of its Agricultural Research Administration, and finally the Director of the USDA Graduate School.

Cardon had been actively involved in FAO meetings since 1943, so his election as Director-General on December 9, 1953, with the support of the Eisenhower Administration, was no particular surprise. He had the reputation of a person with high intellectual and ethical standards; however, the pressures of administering a large organization were apparently the principal cause of his persistent ill health. He resigned as Director-General in April 1956.

COMMISSION ON FERTILIZER. This commission was established by a decision of the FAO Council (q.v.) in 1973. Membership is open to all FAO members-states. Its purpose is to provide a forum for studies and consultations on all problems connected with the use of fertilizers, in particular, prices, demand, supply, export, and import trends. The Commission periodically meets to review the activities of the International Fertilizer

Supply Scheme and of the Fertilizer Programme (q.v.). The 12th session of the commission was scheduled for 1992, but shortage of funds caused its postponement until 1994.

COMMISSION ON PLANT GENETICS RESOURCES, AND THE INTERNATIONAL UNDERTAKING. In order to ensure the unrestricted access of all nations to plant genetic resources of agricultural importance, the 1983 FAO Conference (q.v.), after elaborate planning, adopted an International Undertaking on Plant Genetic Resources. Any government may agree to participate, and those which do set up programs for the purpose of identifying and preserving plant genetic resources that are in danger of becoming extinct or those that might be useful for research and development. Participating governments are committed to allow access to plant genetic resources under their control. Purposes thereof must be scientific research, plant breeding, and genetic resource conservation.

A Commission on Plant Genetics Resources was established in 1983; any FAO member-state may be a member. This Commission is responsible for monitoring the undertaking agreement and for recommending measures which might lead to its improvement. The Commission met first in 1985. At its 4th meeting in 1991, there was considerable discussion of (1) transforming the undertaking into a legally binding agreement and (2) including animal genetics resources as a part of the undertaking. However, the only consensus reached was to review the matter further at a later date.

COMMITTEE ON AGRICULTURE (COAG). This committee was established in 1971 by the Conference (q.v.) and is one of FAO's major policy-recommending committees. Membership is open; any member-state may join, and, by 1986, some 74 had done so. Normally, COAG meets once each biennium, preferably early in a Conference year. It conducts periodic, selective reviews and appraisals of various agricultural and nutritional problems with a view to proposing concerted action by the member-governments. Also, the Committee functions as a kind of consultant to the Council (q.v.) on many agricultural matters, and occasionally conducts oversight of the field programs which came within its jurisdiction. As an example of its achievements, COAG agreed on the need for an International Code of Conduct for the Distribution and Use of Pesticides (q.v.) and the importance of proper training for pesticide users.

COMMITTEE ON COMMODITY PROBLEMS (CCP), INCLUDING THE CONSULTATIVE SUB-COMMITTEE ON SURPLUS DISPOSAL. In 1946, Sir John Orr (later Lord Boyd Orr), the first FAO Director-General (q.v.), proposed to the initial meeting of the FAO Conference (q.v.) in Copenhagen that a World Food Board be established—presumably, but not necessarily, within FAO. The board would have the authority to buy, hold, and sell major agricultural commodities entering world trade, and to set maximum and minimum prices internationally for these commodities. This proposal was defeated. Then, in 1949, Norris E. Dodd (q.v.) (Orr's successor) proposed the creation of an International Commodity Clearing House, which would have functions resulting in FAO's management of a world food reserve. This proposal was rejected by the 1949 FAO Conference.

However, that Conference did mandate the establishment of a (much less powerful) Committee on Commodity Problems. Membership is open to all FAO member-states. The Committee normally meets twice each biennium in Washington, D.C. Its principal functions are to keep under review and survey food commodity problems of an international character and report any recommendations on world food aid issues to a subsequent FAO Council (q.v.).

By 1954, surplus food commodities had become a problem, especially for the United States. In that year the U.S. Congress enacted Public Law 480 (Agricultural Trade Development and Assistance Act; later named The Food for Peace Act of 1966). Fearful that this extensive U.S. food aid program would damage normal world food trade, CCP set up a Consultative Sub-Committee on Surplus Disposal. This Sub-Committee has open membership for FAO member-states, meets some ten times a year in Washington, D.C., and keeps under review—within the terms of its Guidelines and Principles of Surplus Disposal—worldwide food aid activities.

Also, 11 Intergovernmental Groups (IGs) (q.v.) of commodities from bananas to wine are in operation. Membership is open to any member-state that has a particular interest in that commodity. Some IGs are considerably more active and influential than others; each of them reports to the Committee on Commodity Problems.

COMMITTEE ON CONSTITUTIONAL AND LEGAL MATTERS (CCLM). The establishment of this committee is required by Article 5 of the FAO Constitution (q.v.). Its purpose is to consider specific constitutional and legal issues referred to it by the Council (q.v.) or by the Director-General (q.v.). Membership is composed of not more than seven member nations elected for two years by the Council at its session immediately following the regular Conference (q.v.) session. The General Rules specify 12 different functions of CCLM. Its reports and recommendations are forwarded to the Council.

COMMITTEE ON FISHERIES (COFI) AND THE FISH-ERIES DEPARTMENT. In 1965, the Conference (q.v.) upgraded the Fisheries Division into a Fisheries Department. At the same time, a Committee on Fisheries was created, making it a major substantive committee within FAO's organizational structure. Initially a closed committee (first of 30, then 34 member-states) it became open in 1971 to any member-state which desired to participate. Presently the Committee membership is 67. Two meetings are held each biennium.

In the 1950s, six regional intergovernmental commissions were set up as an integral part of FAO to deal with the conservation and rational development of marine resources. In 1982, the United Nations Convention on the Law of the Sea (UNCLOS) recognized the coastal states' authority to manage their fisheries within 200-mile exclusive economic zones. To assist the developing countries in the management of this new and valuable jurisdiction FAO increased its informational, training, and technology responsibilities regarding the growing fishery industry. (See World Conference on Fisheries Management and Development.)

Some 15 subcommittees, commissions, and councils—functional or regional—have been established to advise COFI, and to assist the member-states in the promotion and conservation of their fishing industry.

COMMITTEE ON FORESTRY (COFO). In the planning stage, forestry was not considered to be within FAO's jurisdiction and responsibility. Then, in November 1943, that issue was brought to U.S. President Franklin D. Roosevelt's attention. His scribbled response was: "Yes, I think forestry should be included," and it was.

For several years, there was only a Forestry Division within the Agriculture Department; then, in 1969, it was upgraded to a Forestry Department. In 1971, the Conference (q.v.) agreed to the establishment of a Committee on Forestry. Normally this Committee meets once each biennium, usually in non-Conference years. It is a Committee open to all member-states which desire and decide to join.

Some 12 regional commissions and product committees are operative in assisting and advising COFO, and report periodically to that committee.

COMMITTEE ON WORLD FOOD SECURITY (CFS). This is one of the eight major committees reporting to the FAO Council (q.v.). It is the last in time in that the Committee was not established until 1975. The Committee is clearly the product of the world food crisis of the early 1970s and of the decision by the 1974 World Food Conference (q.v.) (Resolution XVII) to establish an International Undertaking on World Food Security (q.v.), "taking account of its voluntary nature and the sovereign rights of nations," as stimulated in that resolution.

The Committee on World Food Security meets at least twice during every biennium; membership is open to all member-states, and a majority of them are presently members.

The functions of CFS are: (1) to keep under continuous review the world food situation concerning food supplies; (2) to make periodic evaluations of current and prospective world food supplies; (3) to recommend short-term and longer-term policy actions to member-states; and (4) to review actions by governments to implement the International Undertaking on World Food Security (q.v.). (See World Food Security Compact.)

CONFERENCE. The Conference is the sovereign governing body of FAO. It meets in regular session in November of odd-numbered years for three weeks. Each member-state is represented by one delegate, and the decision-making rule is that each member-state has one vote. However, FAO is a consensus-type organization. Very few decisions are decided on the principle of majority rule. Policy differences have almost always been negotiated by the Director-General (q.v.), usually at or before the Council (q.v.) session which meets just prior to the Conference. However, it is important to note that the Conference has the ultimate policy-making and elective authority. Stated succinctly, the Conference has the authority and responsibility to determine the policies and approve the budget of FAO.

CONSTITUTION (BASIC TEXTS, VOLS. I & II, 1992 EDITION). Forty- five member-states were eligible for "original membership" in FAO in 1945. The signing of the Constitution and the opening of the first FAO Conference (q.v.) took place in Quebec, Canada, on October 16, 1945. However, by the close of that Conference only 42 member-states had signed the articles of ratification, not including the Soviet Union.

As of 1992, the *Basic Texts* of FAO constitute a combined, two-volume document of 240 pages. Volume I comprises a 20-page Constitution, 70 pages of General Rules, 20 pages of Financial Regulations, and some 42 pages of Rules of Procedure for the Council and the seven principal committees: Programme, Finance, Commodity Problems, Fisheries, Forestry, Agriculture, and World Food Security.

Volume II is composed of ten sections, including an alphabetical index, totaling 88 pages. For example, one section stipulates the "Authority, terms of Reference and Constitutional Status of Regional Conferences."

Each Conference may amend the Constitution by a two-thirds majority of the votes cast, but this majority must consist of more than one-half of the member-states.

COUNCIL. The first FAO Conference (q.v.) elected a 15-person Executive Committee. The members thereof were selected primarily for their individual competence in matters of agriculture and food, and not as representatives of governments. However, in 1947, the Preparatory Commission on World Food Proposals recommended that the Executive Committee be transformed into an 18-member Council, with balanced geographical representation, and with the members nominated by member-states.

Presently, the Council has 49 members, elected by the Conference (q.v.) for three years, with staggered terms. Each geographic region caucuses at the Conference, and nominates its new members, usually alternating among the countries therein. However, in the North American region there are two members so the United States and Canada are always members of the Council. The membership, by geographic region is as follows:

Africa – 12	Near East – 6
Asia – 9	North America – 2
Europe – 10	Southwest Pacific – 1
Latin America &	
Caribbean – 9	Total = 49

The Council is responsible for functions concerned with the world agriculture and food situation, the current and prospective activities of FAO—including its Programme of Work and Budget (q.v.), financial management, and constitutional matters. Also, the Council may establish commissions, committees, and working parties.

In terms of relative influence, the Council is generally considered to be the most powerful institution in the FAO constitutional hierarchy. It could be, and has been, overruled by a subsequent Conference, but as a useful generalization it could be said: the agreements and compromises worked out by a Council will be ratified at the subsequent Conference.

However, it needs to be remembered that FAO is an international specialized agency, composed of some 160 member-states. FAO resolutions are larded with words, such as "commended," "conceived," "agreed," "supported," and the like. Final authority remains with the individual member-states.

COUNTRY REPRESENTATIVES. A country representative is any appointee of the Director-General (q.v.) to assist him and FAO in the formulation, negotiation, and implementation of country-specific programs. Ostensibly, the FAO country representative is responsible to the UNDP representative, but one of Director-General Saouma's (q.v.) strategies since his election in 1975 has been to establish often a direct FAO-country relationship through the use and activities of the country representative.

Sometimes referred to as FAORs, these country representatives now are assigned to 106 countries, although that covers a few multiple accreditations.

CURRENT AGRICULTURAL RESEARCH INFORMATION SYSTEM (CARIS). This information system provides member-states with a mechanism for the exchange of information about ongoing research activities. In 1978, CARIS produced the first of its worldwide directories covering research institutions, 10,000 research workers, and 3,000 research organizations involved in 20,000 projects. Since 1979, CARIS has been organized in the form of a decentralized network of national and regional centers. However, FAO maintains the global database by merging regional and national files. By 1985, 80 countries had joined the system.

-D-

DIOUF, JACQUES (1938–). On November 8, 1993, Jacques Diouf of Senegal was elected to be the next Director-General of the FAO at the biennial meeting of the FAO Conference (q.v.). It was a well-contested election. There were originally nine candidates nominated by member-states; Diouf was elected on the sixth ballot. His advanced education took place in France, and he received a Ph.D. degree (Social Science of the Rural Sector) from the Faculté de Droit et de Sciences économiques, Sorbonne, Paris. Diouf has served in numerous positions within the Senegal government and African regional organizations, and at the time of his election he was ambassador with the Senegal Permanent Mission to the United Nations in New York.

DIRECTOR-GENERAL (D-G). Students and observers of FAO's activities and polices would likely agree that the Office of Director-General is by far the most powerful position in that international organization. He/she has the principal political relationship with member-states and other international organizations, is the public representative internationally for that organization, provides the public leadership, and exercises administrative leadership and control (e.g., appointments of top-level personnel). On the other hand, the Director-General is an elected office—by the Conference (q.v.), for a six-year term, with each member-state having one vote. Furthermore, the Director-General functions under definite financial constraints; moreover, deficiencies in political will on the part of the member-states seriously limit his/her ability to influence and (especially) control the acceptance of new policies and programs. A Director-General is confronted with a dilemma which appears to be impossible to resolve: how to convince member-states, on a rich-poor continuum, to give legitimacy (acceptance) and financial support to policies and programs which they may not believe to be in their national interest, and then to implement effectively those which the member-states profess to accept but refuse to finance or, quite possibly, to comply with.

It has been said that the ideal D-G should have the worldwide, professional reputation of Lord Boyd Orr (q.v.), the diplomatic and leadership skills of B. R. Sen (q.v.), and the administrative competency of Edouard Saouma (q.v.).

DODD, NORRIS E. (1879–1968). Born and educated in Iowa, Dodd later moved westward, was trained as a pharmacist, established several pharmacies, became a farmer-landowner, and a businessman with numerous investments. In the early New Deal years he became actively involved in the USDA's Agricultural Adjustment Administration and worked his way up through that hierarchy and was eventually appointed U.S. Under Secretary of Agriculture. From that position he moved in 1948 to that of FAO's second Director-General (q.v.). Dodd was well-acquainted with FAO and its policies and programs in that he served as U.S. delegate at two Conference (q.v.) sessions and several of the Council (q.v.) meetings. He was reelected D-G in 1951, but with a change of U.S. Administrations (from Truman, Democrat, to Eisenhower, Republican) he lost his political support. However, he did not leave that office until February 1954.

Dodd was Director-General during the period (February 1951) when FAO was moved from Washington, D.C., to Rome, Italy.

-E-

No entries

-F-

FAO/WHO CODEX ALIMENTARIUS COMMISSION. Jointly with the World Health Organization (WHO), FAO established a Codex Alimentarius Commission in 1961, which had 129 members by 1985. The Commission meets in Rome biennially, but most of the work is carried on through subsidiary bodies, called Codex Committees. These numerous Committees and the parent body deal with food quality standards, including maximum limits for pesticide residues in food, and with food standards for groups of commodities, plus such matters as labeling, methods of analysis and sampling, and veterinary drugs. By 1990, this collection of internationally accepted food standards had resulted in a 30–volume publication. FAO trimmed that collection to a one-volume *Abridged Codex* of some 600 pages.

The Commission is responsible for making proposals to, and is consulted by, the Directors-General (q.v.) of FAO and WHO on all matters pertaining to the implementation of the joint FAO/WHO Food Standards Programme. Membership on the Commission is open to all member-states of those organizations. There is an Executive Committee of eight, elected by the

Commission, one from each major geographic region. The funding for the Commission is a budgeted item in the Regular Programmes of FAO and WHO.

FERTILIZER PROGRAMME. This program was begun in 1961. Its formal objective was "to improve crop production and farmers' incomes through the efficient use of fertilizers." Since its origin the scope of the Programme has broadened to include all aspects of crop production. Funding is largely voluntary, and it is supported by governments, non-governmental organizations (NGOs), and the fertilizer industry. The Programme operates in Third World countries through the use of field trials, field demonstrations, and pilot schemes with an average duration of six years in any single country. In July 1974, FAO created the International Fertilizer Supply Scheme. The Scheme served as a channel for distribution of fertilizers to countries with serious balance of payments problems. In 1986, for example, the Programme was involved in 3,500 field trials and more than 12,000 field demonstrations in developing countries. Now in its 31st year (1993), the Programme functions at a minimal level of activity due to a serious funding shortage.

FIELD PROGRAMME, AND REVIEW OF FIELD PROGRAMME. One of the principal roles of FAO is to promote and provide technical assistance to its member-states. By and large, this means technical assistance to the developing nations, primarily in the form of field projects. Funding for the Field Programme is provided primarily by the United Nations Development Program (UNDP) and Trust Funds (q.v.); the latter are voluntarily supplied by industrial nations. A small percentage comes from FAO's Technical Cooperation Program (TCP) (q.v.), which is funded by the regular budget. For the 1990–91 biennium this meant allocations as follows: UNDP–$176 million, Trust Funds–$195 million, and TCP–$36 million, for a total of $407 million. This permitted a record expenditure toward some 2,300 projects in 140 countries and territories. Keep in mind, however, that field projects are paid for largely from the budgets of participating countries. Total budgets of field projects for 1990–91 were over $2.2 billion.

The biennial review of field programs is presented to each Conference (q.v.) and its preceding Council (q.v.)—e.g., *Review of Field Programmes, 1990–91.* This document is the source of considerable review, discussion, and debate.

FINANCE COMMITTEE. Originally named the Sub-Committee on Finance, then the Committee on Financial Control, in 1958 the Conference (q.v.) upgraded its responsibilities and changed the name to Finance Committee. It is one of the eight constitutionally mandated committees, and is comprised of nine members who are elected by the Conference for two year terms. The election process is a bit complex, but in brief the developing nations are allotted six seats, while Europe, North America, and the Southwest Pacific have three. The committee meets annually, usually concurrently with the Programme Committee (q.v.). Its principal purpose is to assist the Council (q.v.) in exercising control over the financial administration of the FAO. The Committee has some 22 prescribed functions, but essentially it examines carefully the Director-General's Programme of Work and Budget (qq.v.), and then forwards its findings and recommendations to the Council.

FINANCING. Funds for the regular budget are levies on member-states which are based primarily on the Gross

National Product (GNP) of each. However, the United States Congress has legislated that the U.S. contribution may not be more than 25 percent of the regular budget. As examples, for 1992–93, Japan's percentage assessment was 13.32, Nigeria's 0.23, and Niger's 0.1.

Funds for the Field Programme (q.v.) are voluntary contributions to FAO to finance its technical assistance programs. Principal funding sources for the Field Programme are UNDP and Trust Funds (q.v.) from individual member-states.

In recent years the problem of arrears has been serious. As of November 1991, seven member-states were in arrears for over $293 million, which represented 95 percent of the arrears outstanding. Of that amount the United States owed over $116 million.

The following table shows the funds available by selected biennia until 1976. Thereafter the funds are for each biennium to 1992–1993.

Financial Resources Available to FAO for Selected Biennia
(U.S. dollars)

Biennium	Regular Budget	Field Programme (Extra Budgetary Resources)	Total
1946–47	8,361,000	— — — —	8,361,000
1956–57	13,400,000	17,589,000	30,989,000
1966–67	49,974,000	112,039,000	162,013,000
1976–77	167,000,000	389,783,000	556,783,000
1978–79	210,150,000	437,168,000	647,318,000
1980–81	278,740,000	581,120,000	859,860,000
1982–83	386,016,000	683,047,000	1,089,063,000
1984–85	421,627,000	653,502,000	1,075,129,000
1986–87	448,380,000	684,597,000	1,132,977,000
1988–89	451,060,000	714,371,000	1,165,431,000
1990–91	574,460,000	774,762,000	1,349,222,000
1992–93	651,708,000	880,063,000	1,531,771,000

FREEDOM FROM HUNGER CAMPAIGN/ACTION FOR DEVELOPMENT (FFHC/AD). In 1958, Director-General B. R. Sen (qq.v.) proposed the launching of a worldwide campaign to focus attention on the world food problem, and to generate private funds to be used by FAO for the alleviation of that problem. This Freedom from Hunger Campaign (FFHC) became operational in 1959, with the primary objective of assisting individuals, religious groups, and other interested organizations to become involved in attacking the continuing problem of world hunger. This Campaign operates largely through national committees; non-governmental organizations (NGOs) are generally the prime movers.

The Campaign is periodically reviewed by FAO Conferences and is now officially called the Freedom from Hunger Campaign/Action for Development. In its field program, FFHC/AD activities are financed by contributions from NGOs. Special importance is attached to improving the conditions of the rural poor, notably through assisting them to set up their own development organizations.

-G-

GLOBAL INFORMATION AND EARLY WARNING SYSTEM FOR FOOD AND AGRICULTURE (GIEWS). The world food crisis of 1973–74 was further proof that FAO needed to improve substantially its capacity to provide food intelligence information— worldwide, accurate, immediate, up-to-date. GIEWS was credited as a major FAO response to meet this serious shortcoming. Input into this intelligence operation is from member governments, regional organizations and even NGOs. Satellite data, aerial photography and reconnaissance, and other advances in science and technology have become invaluable tools.

Food Outlook reports are issued each month, along with 11 monthly reports on *Food Crops and Shortages.* Field crop assessment missions by the staff have increased significantly; 85 such missions were undertaken in 1990–91.

These activities, among others, have enabled FAO to operate an early food-warning system which functions considerably better than was the situation in 1973.

-H-

No entries

-I-

INTEGRATED PEST MANAGEMENT (IPM). Crop protection from natural pests was among FAO's early priorities, and its importance is rising as the intensification of farming techniques and environmental concerns have acquired momentum. Initially, the main emphasis on protection was for the user of chemical pesticides. In recent years, the possible carcinogenic (cancer producing) effects of pesticides has become a very controversial issue. Pesticides continue to be of primary importance in crop protection, but other techniques, biological rather than chemical, have been increasingly proposed and sometimes utilized—e.g., the introduction of crop pests and the use of so-called trap crops to divert pests from the main harvest. The emphasis is now on Integrated Pest Management (IPM), which means that several biological techniques are used, and the application of pesticides has been kept to a minimum.

In 1965, an FAO symposium on IPM strategies was held, and provisions specifying the use of IPM techniques have been prescribed over the last two decades. However, worldwide fears of increased pesticide use in agriculture led to the proposal of an International Code of Conduct on the Distribution and Use of Pesticides (q.v.).

INTEGRATION OF WOMEN INTO AGRICULTURAL AND RURAL DEVELOPMENT, INCLUDING THE PLAN OF ACTION. One of the major policy issues in FAO during the last few years has revolved around the role of women in agricultural and rural development. At the 1987 Conference (q.v.) the member-states requested that a proposal should be prepared for the following Conference, with the principal thrust of the proposal aimed at raising women's agricultural productivity and income-producing capacity in developing countries. The FAO Secretariat (q.v.) prepared the necessary documents; they were discussed and approved by the Council (q.v.) and forwarded to the 1989 Conference for its decision.

The Plan of Action for the Integration of Women into Agricultural and Rural Development (its official title) was unanimously approved at the 1989 Conference, which also passed a resolution titled: Measures of the Implementation and Follow-Up of the Plan of Action for Integration of Women in Development. It was recognized that of fundamental importance would be the active involvement and support of the member-states in the implementation of the Plan of Action. In this connection, the delegates noted the increasing number of women who are heads of rural households, and underlined the necessity of designing special programs to assist them to be more productive, and to be treated more fairly.

INTERGOVERNMENTAL GROUPS (IGGs) ON: BA-
NANAS, CITRUS FRUITS, COCOA, HARD FI-
BRES, GRAINS, JUTE-KENAF-ALLIED FIBRES,
MEAT, OILSEEDS-OIL-FATS, RICE, TEA, WINE &
WINE PRODUCTS. These 11 Groups are subcommittees of the Committee on Commodity Problems
(q.v.). Membership is open to any FAO member-state.
Each Group meets annually or biennially, although this
varies. Their functions are primarily of a consultative
nature such as discussion of the current economic
problems of the commodity, review of major developments in the world economy, exchange of official
forecasts of export availabilities and import requirements, analysis of selected national policies, etc. These
Groups are sometimes the initial stage in policy developments of a particular commodity. That is, the FAO
Secretariat (q.v.) may suggest a particular policy
change or possible alternative course of action. Such a
proposal may be accepted or modified by the Group,
then reported to the Committee on Commodity Problems, and perhaps on to the Council (q.v.) and the
Conference (q.v.).

INTERLINKED COMPUTER STORAGE AND PRO-
CESSING SYSTEM (ICS). What is being stored and
processed by this system is food and agricultural
commodity data. This includes primary and processed
crops, livestock and fishery products, forestry products,
and agricultural imports (i.e., fertilizers, agricultural
machinery, and other means of production) plus basic
land use, population, and economic data. Since the
World Conference on Agrarian Reform and Rural
Development in 1979, socio-economic indicators have
begun to be incorporated into the system. In conse-
quence, ICS has become the world's premier source of
statistical data on agriculture, fisheries, and forestry.

This has meant that the ICS system has been a principal source for many of the long-range studies on the future of world agriculture. However, a necessary caveat must be noted: ICS can be no more accurate than the data collected by national governments and then transmitted to FAO.

INTERNATIONAL AGRICULTURAL ADJUSTMENT: GUIDELINES AND TARGETS. After the 1974 World Food Conference (q.v.), the FAO Conference (q.v.) agreed on the general outline of an agricultural development strategy based on 12 "guidelines." (Guideline One, for example, was a production growth rate of at least four percent per annum for the developing countries.) Thereafter a progress report was made periodically to the Conference relative to the achievement of the targets and the guidelines. (The seventh *Progress Report* was submitted to the 26th Conference in 1991.) These reports are a useful overview of world food developments during the three-year period of the report.

INTERNATIONAL CODE OF CONDUCT ON THE DISTRIBUTION AND USE OF PESTICIDES, INCLUDING PRIOR INFORMED CONSENT. FAO initiated its pesticide program in 1959 because there was much concern about the possible hazards to human health from pesticide use in agriculture. Over the next 20 years, in close cooperation with the World Health Organization (WHO), committees of experts on pesticides met to evaluate the potential dangers and to recommend possible courses of action. By 1981, a consensus seemed to develop among the member-states that the FAO Secretariat (q.v.) should draft an International Code of Conduct on the Distribution and Use of Pesticides. The draft was approved by the Committee on Agriculture (q.v.) and the FAO Council (q.v.) in 1985 and forwarded to the Conference (q.v.) that same year. There a number of differences and disagreements became evident. In early drafts of the Code there were provisions which embodied the principle referred to as "Prior Informed Consent" (PIC). In brief, the developing nations contended that an industrial country must not sell pesticides to them which were prohibited for sale within that industrial country, without the prior consent of the developing nation. This restriction was unacceptable to some of the industrial countries for economic and political reasons.

A number of revisions and amendments to the Code accrued between 1981 and 1985, so when the 1985 Conference agreed to the Code the PIC provisions were no longer included. The majority of the delegates expressed "deep concern" over this omission. However, the Conference unanimously agreed on the usefulness, timeliness and voluntary nature of the Code, and (as noted in the Conference Report) "most members suggested there be a first revision within the next biennium."

At the 1989 Conference, a compromise was agreed to whereby member-states will notify FAO when they ban or severely restrict use of a pesticide. Thereupon FAO will notify other countries of the action taken. In the first phase of the implementation of the Code, all member-states would be informed by FAO of pesticides which had already been banned or severely restricted in five or more countries.

The UN Environment Program (UNEP) asserted its claim to authority in this issue and by 1989 compatible and complementary proposals for implementing the Code had been agreed to by FAO and UNEP. Since 1992, any newly-banned or severely restricted pesticide is subject to the PIC procedure.

However, it was agreed at the June 1991 meeting of the Council (q.v.) and subsequently at the Conference that it would be "premature" to consider the conversion of the Code into a binding legal instrument. If the majority of the member-states had insisted on doing so it is very likely that no agreement would have been reached.

INTERNATIONAL CONFERENCE ON NUTRITION, AND PLAN OF ACTION. This Conference was organized by FAO and WHO, and held in Rome, Italy, from December 5–11, 1992. The participants were ministers of health (and other like titles) from governments of member-states, with observers from farming, health, industry, and people's organizations. The central aim of the Conference was to persuade the governments of the participants to commit the necessary political will and resources to tackle effectively the problems of hunger and malnutrition. Extensive preparations for the conference were involved: country papers, regional meetings, and in August 1992 a meeting of the Preparatory Committee. Prior to these meetings the joint FAO and WHO Secretariats (q.v.) prepared a global assessment of the current nutritional situation, including studies of policies and programs which have had some considerable success.

The outcome of the Conference was an elaborate statement recommending numerous policies and programs for the alleviation of malnutrition, especially in developing countries. It was stressed, too, that the implementation of the Plan of Action was of special importance and that member-states should give a high priority to the Plan and provide adequate resources for carrying out the necessary programs.

INTERNATIONAL INFORMATION SYSTEM FOR THE AGRICULTURAL SCIENCES AND TECHNOL-

OGY (AGRIS). This is an international cooperative information system which deals with agricultural literature; it is the largest system of its kind in the world. AGRIS became operational in 1975. To date 120 countries and 14 regional and international centers are participating in this network which provides bibliographic references to publications which originate with one of the participants. Each month additions to the bibliography are printed in *Agrindex,* or are available on tapes, along with on-line access. The database has accumulated more than two million entries and is increasing at a rate of about 120,000 new entries each year. Participating countries often take advantage of the extensive advisory and training services which FAO makes available.

INTERNATIONAL UNDERTAKING ON WORLD FOOD SECURITY. World food security has been a principal objective of FAO throughout its (almost) 50-year history. However, the world food crisis of the early 1970s created the political environment from which the rhetoric (adequate food for all people of the world) could be made more explicit in terms of policy and program. During this period the FAO Secretariat (q.v.) formulated a proposal which came to be called officially the International Undertaking on World Food Security. A draft of this proposal was considered by the 1973 FAO Conference (q.v.), and it was decided to submit this draft to the member-states for further consideration. A revised document was adopted by the FAO Council (q.v.) in November 1974, and was endorsed by the World Food Conference (q.v.) that same month (Resolution XVIII). Very briefly, this Undertaking contains a set of general principles for stockholding, special assistance to developing countries, exchange of information, and arrangements for consultations. Member-states were urged to adhere to these principles, but on a voluntary basis.

Then, in November 1975, the FAO Conference established the Committee on World Food Security (q.v.).

During the late 1970s and early 1980s there were considerable diplomatic efforts to obtain an international grains agreement. These efforts did not succeed so Director-General Edouard Saouma (qq.v.) proposed a new and broadened definition of world food security, and his recommendations were adopted by the 1983 FAO Conference. Succinctly, this wider concept placed emphasis on: production, especially by developing countries; stability in the movement of food in international trade; and access to available food stocks by needy, developing nations. This broadened concept is the closest FAO has yet come to adopting a world food policy.

Soon thereafter, in an attempt to renew international resolve to tackle world food security problems, Saouma proposed the adoption of a World Food Security Compact (q.v.). After considerable discussion and some controversy this Compact was adopted at the 1985 FAO Conference. (See Committee on World Food Security and World Food Security Compact.)

-J-

No entries

-K-

No entries

-L-

No entries

-M-

MEDIUM-TERM PLAN, 1992–97. At its 1991 meeting, the FAO Conference (q.v.) received and approved the Medium-Term Plan for 1992–97. This was the reintroduction of a formal, long-term programming process, and its revival had been one of the major recommendations of the 1989 Conference's "Review of Certain Aspects of FAO's Goals and Operations." The Programme and Finance Committees (qq.v.) and the Council (q.v.) had discussed the Medium-Term Plan, and recommended adoption by the 1991 Conference. This document consists of five parts: Overview of Background; Issues, Cross-Sectorial Actions; Programme Priorities; Regional Dimensions; plus Conclusions. It is a rolling plan, advanced and revised every two years by the FAO institutional structure.

The principal controversy at the 1991 Conference centered on the financial resources of future programs. The previous Conference had directed that the Medium-Term Plan should, if possible, include provisional indicators of resources by program. However, for the first biennium (1992–93) the Plan did not indicate any net growth in programs. Many of the delegates from developing countries observed that, in their opinion, this was an inauspicious start for this planning process. However, some of the industrial countries claimed that the budgeting process by their governments made it impossible to agree to any long-term financial commitments. It was agreed by the Conference that these projected budget estimates would be purely indicative projections and would constitute no binding obligation. It was also agreed that the Plan was a key outcome of the FAO Review.

-N-

No entries

-O-

ORR, SIR JOHN BOYD (Lord Boyd Orr) (1880–1971). The first Director-General (q.v.) of FAO, Orr was elected to that office at the first Conference (q.v.) in 1945 and served until 1948. Born in Scotland, he was educated at the University of Glasgow (MD in 1914, D.Sc. in 1920). He was director of the Rowett Research Institute for several years, Professor of Agriculture at the University of Aberdeen, and world famous as a nutritionist. He was knighted Sir John Boyd Orr in 1935 and became Lord Boyd Orr in 1949, the same year that he received the Nobel Peace Prize.

Lord Boyd Orr would still be considered the most prominent person ever to serve as FAO's Director-General. Not only was he present at its creation, he provided the essential leadership in the formation and operation of FAO in its first years. Apparently Orr was a very dominant personality who believed that he knew what should be done to attack successfully the world food problem, and that the member-states would approve and support his policy proposals. A world-renowned scientist, he was only marginally successful as a political administrator. His concept of a World Food Board was brilliantly imaginative, but, for that time, and even now, hopelessly unrealistic.

-P-

PEOPLE'S PARTICIPATION IN RURAL DEVELOP-MENT. The World Conference on Agrarian Reform and Rural Development in 1979 had put special emphasis on the need for more grass-roots, "bottom-up" participation in the development and implementation of rural policies and programs. The general belief was, and is, that more active citizen participation in rural areas would lead to more growth and equity. (By growth was meant a higher rate of agricultural production; by equity, a better redistribution of the benefits of that growth to the rural majority.) How to accomplish this had always led to frustration, conflicts, and contradictions. Also, it was unclear as to what FAO's role should be in this emphasis on grass-roots democracy. FAO's function came to be one of advocate and catalyst, providing technical assistance to the individual governments.

In 1989, the Committee on Agriculture (q.v.) considered a plan of action, a strategy for making operational this people's participation in rural development. The Council (q.v.) twice discussed this plan, recommended some revisions thereto, and forwarded the proposal to the 1991 Conference (q.v.). There was a consensus that participatory democracy is a "long-term process." After some discussion at that meeting, a ten-page Plan of Action was adopted. However, it was recognized by the member-states that the primary responsibility for promoting participation in rural areas was that of the individual governments, with "supplementary support" to be provided by FAO.

PREVENTION OF FOOD LOSSES PROGRAMME (PFL). Statistics on the amount of post-harvest losses, especially from the developing countries, are notoriously difficult to obtain. Nevertheless, these food losses during gathering, storage, and distribution are certainly high, sometimes up to one-third of production. In 1977, FAO set up an Action Programme for the Prevention of Food Losses to assist in the promotion and development of sustainable national post-harvest programs, primarily at the village level, and continued to focus on small farmers and women, especially through farm groups. During 1990, there were 37 operational PFL projects with total budget allocations of $25.8 million, of which 19 were in Africa, seven in Asia and the Pacific, five in Latin America and the Caribbean, and five in the Near East, North Africa, and Europe. Staple foods formed the basis of earlier PFL projects. However, increasing emphasis is now being given to roots, tubers, fruit and vegetables, and efforts continue to be made to integrate pre- and post-harvest factors. Collaboration with the private sector has been initiated in several PFL projects, notably in the manufacturing of post-harvest machinery.

PROGRAMME COMMITTEE. This committee is of major importance in the policy-making process of FAO. It is composed of 11 persons from member-states. The Conference (q.v.) designates which member-states; each member-state selects a person who is expert and experienced in the activities of FAO. Members from the developing nations have the dominant number of members, usually an 8:3 ratio. The main purpose of the Programme Committee is to assist the Council (q.v.) in carrying out its duties regarding the development and implementation of FAO's program. The Committee meets at least once each year. Its provisional agenda is prepared by the Director-General (q.v.), although the

Committee must consider any item referred to it by the Council. Probably the Programme Committee's most important function is its review of the biennial Programme of Work and Budget (q.v.), and its recommendations thereon.

PROGRAMME OF WORK AND BUDGET (PWB), 1992–93. This is FAO's principal planning instrument. The Secretariat (q.v.) is constantly in the process of preparing the next PWB (in this instance, 1994–95) while implementing and administering the current Programme. A draft of the PWB is considered extensively by FAO's hierarchy: Programme and Finance Committees, Council, and then the Conference (qq.v.), the ultimate decision-maker. However, the budget is, by and large, incremental in that few new programs can be advanced currently because of severe budget restraints, and few existing programs are abolished, although they are sometimes cut back due to the current financial situation. A basic proposition is one of: who pays/who receives? The major industrial (OECD) member-states (U.S., Japan, Germany, France, United Kingdom, Italy) were assessed two-thirds of the 1992–93 PWB for the Regular Programme. Who receives?—predominantly the developing member-states.

At the 1991 Conference, the PWB for 1992–93 was believed to be a "balanced compromise," although a majority of the member-states rejected the principle of zero growth; even more, it was agreed that the 1992–93 budget resulted in a negative real growth of four percent. Significantly, according to the *Report* of the 1991 Conference, the United States made a "specific commitment . . . regarding the amounts and timing of its payments relating to current assessments and arrears."

- Q-

No entries.

- R-

REGIONAL FOOD PLAN FOR AFRICA. African countries began to gain their independence in the mid–1950s. Since that time, FAO has accorded African issues a high priority. From the *Africa Survey* of 1961 to the *Regional Food Plan for Africa* in 1978 there were studies which identified the food problems of Africa and suggested ways to alleviate them. In 1976, the Regional FAO Conference for Africa had called for the development of a food plan which if consummated would make Africa south of the Sahara self-sufficient in food within a period of ten years. FAO's *Regional Food Plan for Africa* was categorical in denying that such a goal could be achieved. However, the Plan did set forth a series of recommendations for short-, medium-, and long-range programs and policies. The Plan has been a political success in that the African governments, in various conferences, have adopted many of its features as necessary goals and strategies. Albeit, the political will has not equaled the (undoubted) good intentions, and many, perhaps most, of the recommendations contained in FAO's *Regional Food Plan for Africa* have not been implemented.

REGIONAL OFFICES. FAO's Constitution (q.v.) authorizes the Director-General (q.v.) to establish Regional Offices as he/she may decide, with the approval of the Conference (q.v.). The history of these offices is complex, but in brief Regional Offices are located as follows:

Europe - in Rome, Italy
Near East - in Cairo, Egypt
Asia and the Pacific - in Bangkok, Thailand
Latin America - in Santiago, Chile
North America - in Washington, D.C. (officially a Liaison Office)
Africa - in Accra, Ghana

The functions and importance of these Regional Offices has varied considerably throughout FAO's history. At times there have been efforts to stress the decentralization of FAO's activities, thereby increasing the importance of the Regional Offices. However, there have also been efforts to abolish these bodies. Director-General Edouard Saouma (qq.v.) has emphasized the growth and significance of the office of Country Representative (q.v.) in the developing nations, and has downplayed the role and function of the Regional Offices. The Regional Office in the Near East became the target of a bitter controversy in the late 1970s, following the Camp David Accord between Egypt, Israel and the United States. (For political reasons, Israel is considered to be in the Europe region.) The Arab member-states in the Near East region demanded that the regional office be moved from Cairo. The United States intervened in the dispute, unofficially, with a counter-threat to withdraw from FAO. Finally, the dispute was successfully negotiated; the Near East office was moved to Rome, with costs thereof paid by Saudi Arabia. Then, in 1989, the Conference approved, without controversy, the return of that regional office to Cairo, and Egypt agreed to bear the cost of rehabilitation of the former premises.

REGULAR PROGRAMME, AND REVIEW OF REGULAR PROGRAMME. FAO's Regular Programme constitutes the core of its activities. It is a description, analysis and (selective) evaluation of the operational agricultural, fishery, and forestry programs which have been approved by the various Conferences (q.v.). These programs are funded largely by the contributions of member-states which are levied by a UN prescribed formula. The scale of contributions is based principally on the Gross National Product (GNP) of each member-state.

Since 1978, one of the main responsibilities of the Programme Committee (q.v.), and to hardly a lesser extent the Council (q.v.) and Conference, has been the *Review of the Regular Programme* for the preceding biennium. This document provides an overview of FAO's program implementation for that period, and endeavors to estimate the efficiency and effectiveness of the many programs relative to their objectives and the results achieved.

REVIEW OF FAO'S OBJECTIVES, ROLE, PRIORITIES AND STRATEGIES, AND FAO'S FIELD OPERATIONS. This extensive review of FAO was called for by Resolution 6/87 of the 24th session (November 1987) of the FAO Conference (q.v.). Almost $2 million was budgeted for this study. Independent experts were commissioned to conduct special studies of various aspects of FAO and provide conclusions and recommendations. The Finance and Programme Committees (qq.v.) jointly evaluated these studies and made their own report, then Director-General Edouard Saouma (qq.v.) made an evaluation of the conclusions and recommendations, whereupon the Council (q.v.) reviewed the results and made its own report to the 1989 Conference. Its report noted that the Review included 32 recommendations, and 4 additional recommendations were offered by the Director-General. After extensive consideration by this Conference, and not without considerable disagreement, the initial report of the

Finance and Programme Committees—plus the recommendations of the D-G—were agreed to in Resolution 10/89, with the stipulation that the D-G should report to the 1991 Conference on the implementation of the report.

According to the judgment made by the D-G, only 19 of the 36 recommendations called for additional financial resources, which he estimated would total, tentatively, $26.75 million. Among the recommendations were:

(1) development of a computerized management information system for field operations;
(2) strengthening the monitoring and evaluation of field projects;
(3) training of national staff in project formulation, monitoring and evaluation.

In its Report, the 1991 Conference concluded that the delegates were "generally satisfied with the progress achieved in the implementation of its conclusions on the Review, despite the overall resource limitations."

-S-

SAOUMA, EDOUARD (1926–   ). A citizen of Lebanon, Saouma received his university education in Beirut and France. His first public service positions in agriculture were with the Lebanese government. Saouma's formal association with FAO began in 1962, and from 1976 to 1993 he had been Director-General (q.v.). His third six-year term of office expired in November 1993; in mid–1993 Saouma announced that he would not be a candidate for re-election. He has been a dynamic and aggressive D-G, a man of considerable political abilities, one not without many political supporters—notably among the developing nations, and also not without several political critics—notably among the industrial nations which are less than anxious to support financially his innovative, expensive policy and program proposals.

Saouma initiated (one might argue re-initiated) the Technical Cooperation Programme (q.v.) which provided funds for small research and development programs (less than $400,000 a program), and has kept that decision-making under his personal control. He strengthened considerably the office of FAO Country Representative (q.v.) (some 80 now, in developing countries), and largely controlled their appointment and direction from his office. Both programs are, arguably, valuable both in terms of substance and as evidence of good managerial leadership. Within the FAO Secretariat (q.v.) in Rome, one could fairly characterize his leadership as an amalgam of personal egoism and administrative efficiency.

SECRETARIAT The core of modern government, it has been said, is the bureaucracy. And to that generalization, FAO is certainly no exception, although the term secretariat is a less pejorative term to lay persons. As of December 1991, the FAO Secretariat comprised some 6,401 persons, allocated in general categories as follows:

Professionals/Rome	1,279
General Service Staff, Field	1,796
Professional, Field	1,383
General Service Staff, Rome	1,943
Total	6,401

The general principles of public administration usually apply: hierarchy, appointment, promotion, discipline, etc., with two exceptions of note. One, the Director-General (q.v.) is, by far, the most powerful person in the administrative organization (see Charts and Tables, FAO 2). However, his/her authority is not without restrictions; even the D-G's appointment of a Deputy Director-General is subject to the approval of the Council (q.v.). The D-G's directives on salary levels and recruitment must be approved by the Finance Committee (q.v.). Further, FAO has agreed to adhere to the personnel procedures prescribed by the International Civil Service Commission. Even so, the Director-General constitutes an authority figure within the FAO administrative organization; how authoritarian depends, of course, on the D-G's personality. Director-Generals Sen (q.v.) and Saouma (q.v.) dominated the work within their respective secretariats.

It is also necessary to mention that FAO employs on a contract, limited time basis a few thousand persons for the implementation of field projects. According to Ralph Phillips, 3,774 persons were assigned to field projects as of April 1981. (See the Bibliography for a citation of the Phillips study; it is a classic reference.)

SEED IMPROVEMENT AND DEVELOPMENT PROGRAMME (SIDP). This program was begun in 1973 with the ultimate objective of enabling developing countries to become self-sufficient in seed production. SIDP acts as a focal point in channeling and coordinating technical and financial assistance to developing countries for seed improvement. Financial support is primarily from the UNDP and Trust Fund (q.v.) donors. FAO provides training programs, seed samples for experimental testing, and a computerized Seed Infor-

mation System is operational. During 1990, the FAO's
Seed Exchange and Information Centre helped locate
and distribute seed samples for trial and evaluation to
more than 82 developing countries. Also, technical
back-stopping is given by SIDP to FAO-field projects
on variety evaluation, seed production, processing,
storage, distribution, and quality control. The long-term
objective is the establishment of a sound and comprehensive seed program for the main crops of the developing country concerned.

SEN, BINAY RANJAN (B.R.) (1898–). The first non-
Westerner to be elected Director-General (q.v.), Binay
Ranjan Sen of India, served in that position from 1956
until the end of 1967. He came to FAO after having
performed distinguished service in the Indian diplomatic
corps. Although a citizen of a Third World country, his
nomination was actually sponsored by the British government. Sen was a strong leader, and brought to FAO
political experience, vision, and strong leadership. This
was a period in the history of international organizations
when there was considerable optimism, funding support,
and policy innovation. He initiated the Freedom from
Hunger Campaign (q.v.), a program of fund-raising by
and political support for FAO by voluntary relief organizations. Sen also was a leader in establishing FAO
relationships with the World Bank and major agribusiness industries. His experiences as Director-General are
interestingly presented in his autobiographical study,
Towards a Newer World (1982).

SOIL MAP OF THE WORLD. In conjunction with
UNESCO, in 1961, FAO embarked on the preparation
of a soil map of the world. After 17 years of preparation
the project was completed in 1978—subject, of course,

to periodic revision. Soil cartography had been in a chaotic condition so the most immediate benefit from the map was the formulation and adoption of a common terminology and nomenclature that was acceptable to all cartographers. The objective was to make a first assessment of the production potential of the land resources of the developing countries.

As a follow-up, an Agro-Ecological Systems project was undertaken. It dealt with the rain-fed production potential for 11 crops in developing countries, with the objective of determining their potential population-supporting capacity. One tentative conclusion was that the countries in sub-Saharan Africa, which contain more than 60 percent of the population, will be unable to meet their food needs from low-input systems in the year 2000. Even at high levels of input, two countries will not have the production capacity to feed their populations.

-T-

TECHNICAL COOPERATION PROGRAMME (TCP). This program was created in 1976 to meet more effectively unforeseen and urgent requirements of developing countries by providing limited and short-term assistance in a rapid and flexible way. The TCP program was launched with a budget of $18.5 million for the 1976–77 biennium; by the 1990–91 biennium the budget had increased to $67.8 million. Initially the maximum cost for a TCP project was $250,000, which has now been increased to $400,000.

Two evaluation studies of the TCP program have concluded that the program has, by and large, been successful in the pursuit of its development goals. However, there have been constant charges that the program has certain political ramifications in that, or so some member-states claim, the projects are not subject to acceptance by either the Council (q.v.) or the Conference (q.v.), and that the Director-General (q.v.) uses the program to maintain himself in office.

TROPICAL FORESTRY ACTION PLAN (TFAP). TFAP is one of FAO's highest-priority special action programs. It constitutes the internationally-accepted framework for the conservation and use of forest resources in developing countries. TFAP focuses on the potential of forestry to contribute to income and welfare, particularly in rural areas, based on a sustainable approach to the use of forest products. Special attention in recent years is directed to the alleviation of environmental degradation in forest areas.

FAO's responsibilities are primarily ones of coordination and assistance to field missions. Funds are provided by certain Western European governments, plus Japan. As of May 1991, 84 countries have undertaken, or were in the process of organizing, TFAP programs. Besides its global coordination role, FAO's Forestry Department, through the field program, was the executing agency in 1991 for 25 TFAP projects.

TRUST FUNDS. Trust Funds are voluntary financial contributions by donor, industrial countries to FAO for particular projects or programs, always with the concurrence and involvement of the recipient Third World country. A Trust Fund is a triangular arrangement—a written agreement between the donor country, FAO, and the beneficiary country. FAO is responsible for administering the Trust Fund, but donor countries generally influence, or at least attempt to influence, the structure, objectives, and implementation of a particular project. The Trust Fund process is sometimes referred to as the multibilateral option. FAO is a major user of the Trust Fund arrangement, although its use contains within itself the possibility of turning FAO into a service management agency for donor countries.

-U-

No entries

-V-

No entries

-W-

WORLD AGRICULTURE: TOWARD 2000. This FAO study has been well-received by U.S. agricultural economists. A draft *(Agriculture: Toward 2000)* was debated at the 1979 FAO Conference (q.v.), when published in 1981, under a new title, with minor amendments. A revision, consisting mostly of an updating, was published in 1988.

One principal finding of the study was that by the year 2000 a world population of more than six billion persons will require an agricultural output some 50–60 percent greater than that produced in 1980. Forestry and fishery policy analyses were included, too.

A follow-up study—*European Agriculture*—was published in 1990. Despite the title, this study also included North American agriculture. Regarding policy issues, only crops and livestock sectors were included. The new states of Eastern Europe were an important part of the study, but their inclusion caused the findings to be more tentative and speculative.

WORLD CONFERENCE ON AGRARIAN REFORM AND RURAL DEVELOPMENT (WCARRD). This conference was held in Rome, Italy, at the headquarters of the FAO from July 12–20, 1979, and constitutes one of that organization's major accomplishments. The general theme of WCARRD was ''growth with equity and participation.'' Forthcoming from that theme and the Conference proceedings was a Declaration of Principles and a Programme of Action which continue to be an important source of agenda-setting and policy formulation within FAO. The Programme of Action also sets up a monitoring system, and every four years the Conference (q.v.) carries on an extended debate concerning the implementation of the Programme of Action. One of the seven sections of that Programme of Action recognized the fundamental importance of education, training, and extension services in rural areas. The role of women in rural development was also emphasized, as was the significance of improved international trade for the achievement of rural development goals. Unfortunately, national governments have often been less than impressive in the way they have carried out the proposed policies and programs which were formulated in the Programme of Action. The 1991 Conference observed in its *Report* that ''the total number of rural poor has increased between 1980 and 1987,'' and that ''much more [is] needed to be done to promote growth with equity and to alleviate rural poverty.''

WORLD CONFERENCE ON FISHERIES MANAGEMENT AND DEVELOPMENT. This Conference, held in Rome in 1984, brought together the largest number of delegates ever assembled at a high policy level to consider the issues facing the fishery industry. After agreeing on a set of long-term objectives, the Conference endorsed a Strategy for Fisheries Management and Development. Also approved were five directly related Programmes of Action. Periodically (1987 and 1991) the FAO Conference (q.v.) reviewed the progress which had taken place relative to the implementation of the fisheries Strategy and the Programmes of Action. At the 1991 Conference, FAO's key role in providing training and advice in this sector to developing nations was reaffirmed. An overview of the decade of developments since adoption of the United Nations Convention on the Law of the Sea (UNCLOS) is a special chapter in FAO's annual publication, *The State of Food and Agriculture.*

WORLD FOOD CONFERENCE. This conference was held in Rome, Italy, from November 5–16, 1974, but it was not sponsored by FAO. In October 1973, the UN Economic and Social Council recommended to the UN General Assembly that it issue a call for the convening of a world food conference, which the General Assembly proceeded to do. In the following month, the FAO Conference (q.v.) gave this matter its priority consideration, and subsequently its full support. Most of the specialized studies which were examined and acted on by the conference delegates (who represented all sovereign states, including the Soviet Union, Ukraine, and Byelorussia) were the product of FAO. Of continuing value is the study entitled *Assessment of the World Food Situation: Present and Future.*

This was the most important world food conference ever held, a world class event. Much debate, discussion, and dissent were generated by liberal and radical non-governmental organizations, and by many of the delegates from the developing nations. The stature and reputation of FAO were harmed by this Conference. An often-heard criticism, although probably unfair, was to the effect: If FAO had been doing its job effectively this world crisis would never have occurred.

The Conference proceedings resulted in the Declaration on the Eradication of Hunger and Malnutrition, which included the memorable phrase that ''every man, woman and child had the inalienable right to be free from hunger and malnutrition in order to develop fully and maintain their physical and mental facilities.'' More pragmatically, the Conference agreed on a Programme of Action which consisted primarily of 22 resolutions (e.g., ''objectives and strategies of food production'' and ''priorities for agricultural and rural development''). By and large, these resolutions still constitute the world food agenda of today.

Also, the conference delegates decided, after considerable political controversy, that two new food agencies would be created: the World Food Council and the International Fund for Agricultural Development.

WORLD FOOD CONGRESS(ES). The first World Food Congress was held in 1963 in Washington, D.C., to celebrate the 20th anniversary of the historic meeting at Hot Springs, Virginia, which led to the founding of the Food and Agriculture Organization. This Congress was sponsored by the Freedom from Hunger Campaign (FFHC) (q.v.), and it was organized as a ''people to people'' meeting, not as an intergovernmental conference. U.S. President John F. Kennedy addressed the Congress and this phrase from his address has been accorded historic status: ''We have the means, we have the capacity to eliminate hunger from the face of the earth in our lifetime. We need only the will.'' The Congress reviewed current thinking about the world food problem, and issued several recommendations as to what should be done, culminating in a Declaration expressing high intentions.

The second World Food Congress was held at The Hague, Netherlands, in June 1970, with some 1,800 persons in attendance. At this conference, the meetings were not predominantly technical; much of the debate was concerned with the issue of social justice. It was remarkable more for protest than practical action, one more directed at the plight of the rural poor and the role of women in development than the increase of food production.

WORLD FOOD DAY. Since 1979, October 16th (FAO's founding date) has been declared World Food Day in nearly every country. By 1981, more than 140 member-states were observing that event. It has been a propagandistic success for FAO. Each country decides if and how the Day will be celebrated. Whatever the means used, the special attention of local publics is drawn to the plight of millions who live in conditions of poverty, hunger, and misery in its many manifestations. FAO itself offers small amounts of promotional and informational materials to participating countries, if they so desire, and endeavors to promote a general unity of action within the broad limits stipulated by varying cultures and circumstances.

WORLD FOOD SECURITY COMPACT. At the 8th session of the Committee on World Food Security (q.v.), Director-General Edouard Saouma (qq.v.) submitted a proposal for what came to be the World Food Security Compact. After considerable discussion at that Committee's 9th and 10th sessions, a draft compact was approved and submitted to the Council (q.v.). Further dispute was encountered there, but it was finally approved by the 87th

Council and forwarded to the Conference (q.v.) in 1985. The main aim of the Compact was to reaffirm a moral commitment to achieve the objective of ensuring ''that all people at all times are in a position to produce or procure the basic food they need,'' as stated in the Compact, article II, clause 1. The Compact does not involve any new financial or legal commitments on the part of member-states and is strictly voluntary in nature.

In November 1985, the Conference agreed to the adoption of the Compact. However, three delegations (Australia, Canada, and the United States) dissociated their governments from the text of the Compact. Briefly, their reservations were based on the following objections: (1) more consultations should have been held before the Compact was adopted; and (2) the text of the Compact should have been more explicit as to its voluntary, non-binding nature.

WORLD FOOD SURVEY(S). FAO's first *World Food Survey* was published in July 1948, some nine months after the founding of the organization. The official purpose of the survey was, and continues to be, the gathering of ''facts and figures'' concerning hunger and malnutrition worldwide. By 1985, five *World Food Survey*(s) had been conducted and published, one (roughly) about every ten years. Immense difficulties have been encountered—the definition of terms, the gathering of data, the interpretation of what the data mean. With each *Survey,* the quality of the data has improved, as have the methods for analyzing them. There have been critics in abundance. The results, as viewed officially, have been both positive and negative. It would seem that the numbers of those who should be classified as undernourished have remained fairly constant. Perhaps the conclusion reached by the third *World Food Survey* (1963) still holds fairly true: some 10–15 percent of the world's population were undernourished, and about half of those undernourished suffered from hunger or malnutrition or both. Nevertheless, the percentage seems to have remained fairly constant, and in that 30-year period the world's population has increased by 1.5 billion persons.

WORLD SOIL CHARACTER. As viewed by FAO, soil damage and depletion is regarded as the number one environmental problem in many parts of the world. The 1974 World Food Conference (q.v.) had also reached this conclusion and had recommended that FAO prepare what has come to be called a World Food Charter. This was accomplished by the FAO Secretariat (q.v.), and then ultimately approved by the 1981 Conference (q.v.). The Charter is a description and analysis of the world soils, but it is perhaps even more a plan of action. It proposes a general policy framework for member-states to use in setting up programs of soil conservation and reclamation, plus recommendations as to how these programs should be implemented.

-X-

No entries

-Y-

No entries

-Z-

No entries

B. WORLD FOOD PROGRAMME (WFP)

-A-

AQUINO, FRANCISCO (1919–). A citizen of El Salvador, Aquino received his college education at the College for Agronomic Studies in El Salvador and at Harvard University. Thereafter, he served as an agricultural engineer and an economist in numerous public research and advisory positions. From 1956–61, Aquino was in the employ of FAO (q.v.). Later, he had assignments with the World Bank, International Monetary Fund and Inter-American Bank. Thereafter, he became the second Executive Director (q.v.) of the World Food Programme from 1968–76.

-B-

BERTINI, CATHERINE (1950–). A citizen of the United States, she became an Assistant Secretary of Agriculture for Food and Consumer Services during the Bush Administration. In this position, Bertini was responsible for 13 food assistance programs, including the Food Stamp Program, the National School Lunch and Breakfast Programs, and the Women, Infants and Children (WIC) Program. As Assistant Secretary of Agriculture, she was responsible for coordinating nutrition monitoring, nutrition education, and consumer affairs. On April 6, 1992, Bertini became WFP's Executive Director (q.v.), the first woman to hold this position.

BOERMA, ADDEKE HENDRICK (1912–1992). Boerma was first Executive Director (q.v.) of the World Food Programme from 1962–67. He resigned that position to become the Director-General of the Food and Agriculture Organization (FAO). (See his biographical sketch in the FAO section).

-C-

COMMITTEE ON FOOD AID POLICIES AND PROGRAMMES (CFA). The Committee on Food Aid Policies and Programmes is WFP's governing body and also a forum for intergovernmental consultations on all food aid. It normally meets twice a year.

CFA provides general guidance on the policies, administration and operation of the Programme; examines and approves WFP assistance for development and protracted refugee and displaced person projects; reviews the execution of these projects and emergency operations supported by the Programme; and approves WFP's program support and administrative budget.

In its wider function, CFA discusses national and international food aid programs and policies, and formulates proposals for more effective coordination of multilateral, bilateral, and non-governmental food aid programs, including emergency food aid.

Countries are elected to the 42–member CFA for a three-year term, after which they are eligible for reelection. Half are elected by the UN Economic and Social Council (ECOSOC) and half by the FAO Council (q.v.). Twenty-nine of the members represent developing countries, 13 the industrial countries.

As a result of elections held by ECOSOC and the FAO Council in 1992, the membership of CFA in 1993 was as follows:

Term of office expiring	Elected by ECOSOC	Elected by FAO Council
December 31, 1993	Belgium	Argentina
	Egypt	Brazil
	El Salvador	Burundi
	Indonesia	China
	Japan	Netherlands
	Pakistan	Saudi Arabia
	Sweden	Tanzania
December 31, 1994	Colombia	Angola
	Cuba	Cameroon
	Ethiopia	France
	Ghana	Germany
	Norway	Democratic People's Republic of Korea
	Syria	Mexico
	United Kingdom	Romania
December 31, 1995	Denmark	Australia*
	Dominican Republic*	Bangladesh*
	Hungary*	Burkina Faso
	India*	Canada*
	Italy*	Senegal
	Niger	Sri Lanka*
	Nigeria	United States of America*

*Reelected.

-D-

No entries.

-E-

EXECUTIVE DIRECTOR. The Secretariat of the World Food Programme is led by an Executive Director who is responsible and accountable to the Committee on Food Aid (CFA) (q.v.) for the administration of the Programme. She (Catherine Bertini [q.v.] now holds this position as of 1992) was appointed for a five-year term, by agreement of the UN Secretary-General and FAO Director-General (q.v.), after consultation with CFA. She is responsible for the operations of the Secretariat, and for its staffing and organization. The selection and appointment of senior (above the level of D–2) officials in the Secretariat requires the agreement of the UN Secretary-General and FAO Director-General.

-F-

FINANCING. WFP is financed through voluntary contributions by member-countries. Any sovereign state is eligible to be a member of its governing body, the Committee on Food Policies and Programmes (CFA) (q.v.), make a voluntary financial contribution, or attend CFA semi-annual sessions as an observer, if it is not a member of CFA at that time. Contributions are predominantly in the form of cereals (wheat, primarily; also rice and coarse grains) although there is a sizable contribution in dairy products. The General Regulations (q.v.) dictate that 30 percent of the contribution is to be in the form of cash; the table below indicates that this goal was met in 1991–92. However, the WFP Secretariat is generally concerned over shortages in cash for the financing of its obligations.

Biennial targets are first proposed by the Executive Director (q.v.); the proposed target for 1993–94 is $1.5 billion. This target is discussed at length by CFA, which will very likely approve that figure. The Group of 77 members will complain that the target is too low; the OECD members will object and complain about the tight budget situation in their home countries and defend the status quo.

In overview at least, Table A (opposite) comparing "targets and achievements" can rather easily be interpreted. Note that the data include contributions only until February 15, 1993; by the end of 1993 it is likely that the percentage of contributions will have increased to 86–87 percent, or thereabouts. (All of the data which follow are extracted from CFA documents.)

Table B (page 85) lists the country donors for the 1991–92 biennium, again as of December 31, 1991. Only the 26 donors which pledged over one million dollars are listed. However, 58 countries made pledges in some amount; there were also very small contributions by UN agencies and NGOs. (Indeed, "individuals" contributed $28,000 in non-food items!) These donations totaled over $1.9 billion, so they include contributions for emergency projects and the International Emergency Food Reserve (q.v.). However, WFP was responsible for administering this total amount. CEC means Commission of the European Communities, and it should be noted that several member-states of the EC also make sizable donations.

Table C (page 86) is a very brief overview of WFP expenditures during the years, 1986–1992. For the Regular Programme project costs have actually declined. There have been dramatic increases in refugee and emergency operations; also, donors (primarily OECD countries) increasingly request WFP to administer their bilateral projects. This means, of course, that WFP has declining resources to allocate to its primary mission; namely, the use of food as a development tool in low-income countries.

FOOD AID—BILATERAL AND MULTILATERAL. Bilateral food aid is usually contributed through a donor (industrial country) to recipient (a developing country) agreement. WFP is by far the main channel for multilat-

(A) WFP REGULAR PLEDGE POSITION SINCE 1983–84 (AS OF FEBRUARY 15, 1993) (US$ millions)

Period	Commodity	Cash and services	Total	Target	% of target realized	Cash and services as % of total
1983–84	771.6	239.4	1011.0	1200	84	23.7
1985–86	915.7	255.7	1171.4	1350	87	21.8
1987–88	943.4	293.3	1236.7	1400	88	23.7
1989–90	905.8	298.2	1204.0	1400	86	24.7
1991–92	802.7	349.7	1152.4	1500	77	30.3

(B) MAJOR DONORS TO WFP, BIENNIUM 1991–92, AS OF DECEMBER 31, 1991 (US$ thousands)

Total

Rank	Donor	Value	Rank	Donor	Value
1	USA	585,087	14	Italy	17,405
2	CEC	342,139	15	Saudi Arabia	15,000
3	Canada	282,790	16	France	14,397
4	Finland	93,662	17	Austria	7,500
5	Netherlands	84,515	18	Belgium	5,349
6	Norway	77,434	19	Argentina	5,250
7	Denmark	77,006	20	Cuba	2,400
8	Germany	75,241	21	China	2,000
9	Sweden	66,655	22	India	1,920
10	Australia	49,667	23	NGOs	1,361
11	Japan	42,175	24	UN Agencies	1,103
12	Switzerland	34,533	25	Ireland	1,098
13	UK	30,341	26	Pakistan	1,040

(C) WORLD FOOD PROGRAMME HISTORY OF EXPENDITURES (US$ millions)

	1986	1987	1988	1989	1990	1991	1992
Regular Programme							
Projects	517.0	567.3	704.0	566.6	506.1	535.0	488.1
PSA (1)	52.6	55.6	64.0	70.0	75.2	81.8	93.9
Other	1.5	7.9	1.5	1.6	3.1	6.1	4.0
Total Regular Programme	**571.1**	**630.8**	**769.5**	**638.2**	**584.4**	**622.9**	**586.0**
Refugee operations	.0	.0	.0	54.0	171.4	316.7	422.6
Emergency operations	125.4	147.2	174.0	140.8	72.8	226.0	429.7
Bilateral operations	59.0	54.8	122.1	139.8	128.4	150.8	176.0
Other activities	41.5	22.5	42.8	21.9	68.7	115.4	80.6
Total	**797.0**	**855.3**	**1108.4**	**994.7**	**1025.7**	**1431.8**	**1685.9**

(1) Programme Support and Administrative Budget

eral food aid, with a very small proportion provided by UNHCR and other United Nations agencies. Table D (page 88) is extracted from a CFA document. It indicates, inter alia, that over 25 percent of all food aid was provided multilaterally in 1992. The proportion channeled multilaterally increased to a record 28 percent of total deliveries, cereals and non-cereals. This increase is explained by the large volume of relief food aid for which the multilateral share is traditionally much higher.

NGOs (non-governmental organizations; e.g., CARE and OXFAM) contract for and implement some of the bilateral projects, as the table indicates, and their involvement is increasing.

FOOD AID—NEEDS BY 2000. There are strong indications that food aid, multilateral and bilateral, will be needed on an increasing scale during the decade of the 1990s. Much depends of course, on the magnitude of emergency food aid requirements.

Annual cereal imports of developing countries are projected by WFP to increase from about 100 million tons during the mid–1980s—of which about 12 million tons were met by food aid deliveries—to between 145 and 168 million tons by the year 2000. If per capita cereal consumption in the 55 low-income countries that receive between 80 and 90 percent of global food aid were to be maintained at the average level prevailing over the period 1980–89, an estimated 16 million tons of food aid would be required annually in addition to local production and commercially affordable imports.

These projections reflect only anticipated growth in effective market demand. They do not include the food needs of undernourished people who do not have the purchasing power to obtain an adequate diet. To meet minimum caloric standards an estimated 28 million tons of food aid should be supplied annually.

(D) Food Aid—Bilateral and Multilateral (share of total deliveries - %)

Channel	1988	1989	1990	1991	1992
Cereals					
Bilateral	80	82	84	77	74
Government to Government	(71)	(72)	(71)	(65)	(59)
Through NGOs	(9)	(10)	(12)	(11)	(14)
NGOs (own resources)	0.4	0.4	0.6	0.5	0.7
Multilateral	20	17	16	23	25
Non-Cereals					
Bilateral	80	71	74	68	70
Government to Government	(68)	(58)	(55)	(42)	(48)
Through NGOs	(12)	(13)	(19)	(26)	(21)
NGOs (own resources)	0.2	0.4	1.0	0.5	0.4
Multilateral	20	29	25	31	30

In 1991, the Committee on Food Aid Policy and Programmes (q.v.) initiated a series of studies of future aid policies and programs and the role of WFP. A study by Raymond Hopkins, of Swarthmore College, suggested a sharper focus for WFP in light of its major strengths and the most important current and potential constraints it faced. A second study by FAO analyzed factors that may affect food aid needs and availabilities and made policy recommendations on the programming, allocation and use of food aid. A third joint World Bank and WFP study on food aid in Africa, reflected their shared belief that food aid was an important and undervalued resource for development in that region. It concluded that food aid was a significant development resource with special advantages in sustaining a poverty focus, supporting food security, and reducing the social costs of economic adjustment measures.

A study of Danish food aid concluded that food aid had contributed to increased economic growth and reduced poverty in transferring resources to recipient countries. The study also observed that food aid supplies were unlikely to meet increasing food aid needs, which were expected to rise rapidly during the 1990s. Such projections are, of course, based on assumptions which may or may not prove accurate. But the evidence is very persuasive that food aid needs by 2000 will be considerably higher than the 10,000 ton goal set at the 1974 World Food Conference(q.v.).

FOOD AID CONVENTION (FAC). The FAC was originally a part of the International Wheat Agreement of 1971. For political reasons, it is now a separate, binding instrument under which donors mutually pledge amounts of food grain they will contribute to developing countries. The minimum level of aggregate contributions for the current FAC (Food Aid Convention of 1980) is 7.76 million tons of cereals, of which the U.S. commitment is about 4.5 million tons.

The coordination and monitoring of the FAC is done by a Food Aid Committee within the International Wheat Council. The principal purpose of the FAC has been to establish a minimum food security base to protect developing nations from serious food aid shortages. Its mandatory features have been of some use in achieving that goal but the Food Aid Convention probably needs to be substantially updated. Albeit, the major donors oppose an increase in obligations which they would be legally expected to comply with.

Perhaps it should be noted that the U.S. contribution to the FAC does not represent a net addition to its annual food aid contribution; this food would have been contributed in any event.

FOOD AID DONORS. Overseas food assistance following World War II and up until 1965 was almost the exclusive domain of the United States. In 1963, for example, the U.S. food aid contribution was 96 percent of the total. However, by 1975, the U.S. share had declined to some 58 percent of total food aid. The European Community's Common Agricultural Policy (CAP) has proven to be remarkably successful in one sense; that is, it has been a major factor in transforming the EC member-states from largely food importers to highly subsidized food exporters. This CAP program has proved to be immensely expensive, sometimes accounting for 60–70 percent of EC expenditures. On the other hand, the surplus farm commodities could be used by, and were often allocated to, WFP.

Consequently, the total contributions by the European Community to WFP for the 1991–92 biennium, plus the contributions by each of the 12 member-states, were almost $1.1 billion, as compared to just over $1 billion for the United States.

FOOD AID RECIPIENTS. During the last three decades (1963–93), WFP has delivered some $13 billion dollars, involving more than 40 million tons of food, to developing countries to promote economic and social development, and for refugee operations. (See Charts and Tables, WFP 2.)

These food aid commitments to major geographic regions have varied considerably during that period. In the 1963–72 period, some 42 percent of total food aid went to countries of North Africa and the Middle East, and 27 percent to Asian and Pacific countries. By 1979, 48 percent of food aid went to the latter, and only 12 percent to the former.

FOOD AID TO SUB-SAHARAN AFRICA. Food aid to sub-Saharan Africa as a percentage of the total (multilateral and bilateral) has varied in dollar value from 16 percent in the 1963–72 period to 40 percent by 1992. Nearly 60 percent of all WFP food assistance in 1992 (over 5.2 million tons) went to that region for victims of natural and man-made disaster—refugees, displaced persons, and those affected by severe drought. Eight African countries—Ethiopia, Sudan, Zimbabwe, Zambia, Malawi, Kenya, Somalia, and Mozambique—together received almost 80 percent of those food aid deliveries.

In early 1992 it rapidly became evident that the southern Africa region was experiencing one of the worst droughts in recent history. The United Nations Drought Emergency in Southern Appeal called for some 1.78 million tons of food for free distribution and an additional 2.54 million tons of program food aid for subsidized sales within those countries. WFP had the lead role in this effort to provide food to nearly 18 million people who were at risk from starvation in the region.

-G-

GENERAL REGULATIONS. Since its origin in 1969, WFP has always been a joint program of the United Nations and FAO. In pursuance of the provisions of several United Nations General Assembly resolutions, and several resolutions of FAO Conferences, procedures and arrangements for the operation of WFP—in the form of a set of General Regulations—have been formulated by WFP and subsequently approved by the UN's Economic and Social Council (ECOSOC) and FAO's Council (q.v.).

This arrangement required WFP to consult with and, on certain issues, have the approval of the FAO's Director-General (q.v.) before acting. This situation caused numerous FAO/WFP controversies over the years. In the past, there was a clash of leadership personalities, but the disagreements sometimes constituted an operational impediment. After festering for several years, the central issues were resolved in 1991, and WFP's General Regulations were considerably revised, much to WFP's advantage. These revised General Regulations were then endorsed by ECOSOC and the FAO Council. They entered into force on January 1, 1992, in accordance with the provisions of UN General Assembly resolution 46/22 (December 1991) and FAO Conference resolution 9/91 (November 1991). The General Regulations now constitute a document of 12 pages.

GENERAL REGULATIONS, CHANGES IN. The issue of governance of the World Food Programme, which dominated the work of its governing body, the Committee on Food Aid Policies and Programmes (CFA) (q.v.), during 1990, was resolved in 1991. The report of the first Special Session of CFA containing a draft of revised General Regulations (q.v.) of the Programme was submitted to the 99th Session of the FAO Council (q.v.) held in June, and then to the summer session of the Economic and Social Council (ECOSOC). Both endorsed the changes and forwarded them to the FAO Conference (q.v.) and the United Nations General Assembly respectively, for final approval which came toward the end of the year. The changes came into effect at the beginning of 1992.

This straightforward account is factually accurate, but not really descriptive of the political controversy which was involved. For several years the (then) WFP Executive Director James Ingram (qq.v.), had chafed and complained over what he considered to be the excessive involvement of FAO—more personally, the Director-General (q.v.)—in policy-making and decision-making of WFP. Without recounting the specifics, it should be noted that Edouard Saouma (q.v.) did have a certain amount of authority in matters regarding WFP; to an extent, WFP was a subordinate organization responsible to FAO and the United Nations. However, in the minds of Ingram and the WFP bureaucracy, Saouma had become a meddler and an obstructionist, a type of bureaucratic authoritarian. Whatever the truth of this matter, the issue of governance dominated the work of its governing body (CFA) during 1990. The controversy was finally resolved largely in favor of Ingram and WFP. As reported in a CFA document, the following changes were brought about by the revision of WFP's General Regulations:

(1) CFA was enlarged from 30 to 42 members and its composition was changed from an equal representation between developing countries and more economically developed countries to one in which developing countries have 27 members and more economically developed countries 15 members.

(2) CFA now exercises full inter-governmental supervision and direction for all aspects of the Programme, including Food Aid (q.v.) policy, administration, operations, funds and finances.

(3) Responsibility for the administration of the former WFP Trust Fund, now called the WFP Fund, was transferred from the FAO Director-General to the WFP Executive Director, who is accountable to CFA for the management of the Fund. In this context the Programme now has its own financial regulations to govern its operations.

(4) Governments seeking emergency assistance now address requests to the WFP Representative in the country concerned. The Executive Director, after consultations with FAO and other relevant agencies, decides on requests up to the level of authority delegated to him/her to approve development projects (now $1.5 million). In cases of emergency requests exceeding the Executive Director's authority, approval is made jointly by the WFP Executive Director and the FAO Director-General. Previously all emergency operations involving use of WFP resources were approved by the FAO Director-General upon recommendation by the Executive Director.

(5) The Programme now has the authority to contract, acquire and dispose of property and be party to judicial proceedings.

(6) The Executive Director is now accountable to CFA for all aspects of the Programme. The Executive Director's authority on financial and operational

matters, including appointment of staff up to and including the level of D–2, has been increased, corresponding to the greater responsibilities vested in the position.

-H-

No entries

-I-

IMMEDIATE RESPONSE ACCOUNT (IRA). For several years WFP has needed to provide a quick response to new emergency situations by buying food locally or from the nearest commercial source. WFP cash resources are not sufficient to cover immediate food purchases as a regular alternative to borrowing.

In order to remedy this problem, the Committee on Food Aid Policies and Programmes (CFA) (q.v.) in 1991 approved the establishment of a cash account, to be known as the Immediate Response Account, as an integral part of the International Emergency Food Reserve (IEFR) (q.v.). The IRA will be used mainly to buy and deliver food to permit the fastest possible initial response to new emergency situations.

The IRA will be funded by an amount to be set aside annually by CFA from WFP's regular resources ($7.5 million in 1992) and by voluntary contributions from IEFR contributors in convertible currencies free of restrictions as to their use. An annual minimum target of $30 million has been set.

INGRAM, JAMES C. (1928–). A citizen of Australia, Ingram is a graduate of the University of Melbourne in economics and political science. He has had a distinguished career with the Australian government's Department of Foreign Affairs. In 1974, Ingram transferred to the Australian Development Assistance Agency, and later became the Director of the Australian Development Assistance Bureau. In that position he was responsible for the planning and administration of the Australian Overseas Aid Programme. Ingram became WFP's Executive Director (q.v.) on April 1, 1982, was reappointed for a second five-year term in 1987, and voluntarily retired at the conclusion of that term.

INTERNATIONAL EMERGENCY FOOD RESERVE (IEFR). IEFR had its origins in Resolution XVII of the World Food Conference (q.v.) in 1974 and the International Undertaking on World Food Security (q.v.) of the same year. At the UN General Assembly in September 1975, a resolution was adopted more specifically referring to an emergency reserve stock of 500,000 tons to be earmarked and placed at the disposal of WFP to strengthen its capacity to respond to emergency needs. IEFR operates under WFP's administration, supplementing food pledged to WFP's regular operations.

Although WFP is charged with administering the IEFR, it remains dependent on voluntary contributions by donor governments. Moreover, some of the commodities committed to IEFR are directed to particular recipients by the donor governments and only the remainder goes through WFP unrestricted.

In recent years, the 500,000 ton target has become a base (minimum) goal. Due to several protracted and emergency relief conditions, especially in Africa, food commodities requested for IEFR have increased dramatically in volume and value. In 1992, almost 1.4 million tons were contributed, all by OECD countries. Also, in that year a cash account, known as the

Immediate Response Account (IRA) (q.v.), was established by WFP. The IRA is now an integral part of IEFR and is used for the purchase and delivery of emergency food aid for food shortage situations. (See Immediate Response Account.)

INTERNATIONAL FOOD AID INFORMATION SYSTEM (INTERFAIS). This information system, devised and operated by WFP, has become the most comprehensive source of data on all aspects of Food Aid (q.v.) operations. Established in 1987, it provides a monitoring system for worldwide food aid flows in support of operational food aid coordination. This includes delivery schedules, funding sources and channels, supply modes, food aid types, and specific commodities for each individual shipment or purchase.

The database is used to respond to regular queries by food aid administrators to assist their allocation and scheduling processes. It is updated on a continuous basis with data collected from donors, channeling agencies and recipient countries. It is also used to provide statistics for analyses of a variety of food aid policy issues and is the main source of data for many WFP documents. Reports on current food aid flows, schedules and relevant logistics are included in a quarterly WFP publication, the *Food Aid Monitor.*

-J-

No entries

-K-

No entries

-L-

LOCAL PURCHASES. Local purchases, in which food is used by WFP in the same country where it is purchased, have become an important feature of WFP operations. These purchases have to be managed carefully in that they could be harmful to the interests of the developing country. However, a surplus in one region may be able to alleviate a serious demand situation in another region of the same country. And, overall, the purchases will most likely enhance the national economy.

WFP is the largest single purchaser of food in developing countries for use as Food Aid (q.v.).

-M-

MEMORANDUM OF UNDERSTANDING BETWEEN WFP AND UNHCR. In 1991, WFP and UNHCR negotiated a working arrangement which came into effect in 1992. Under this agreement WFP has become the only multilateral channel for Food Aid (q.v.) to developing countries. WFP assumed full responsibility for mobilization of all basic food commodities and the cash resources for meeting transport costs for all UNHCR-managed refugee feeding operations in developing countries involving more than 1,000 beneficiaries.

MONETIZATION OF FOOD AID. The monetization of food aid may be defined as the selling of donated food by WFP and the use of those proceeds by WFP for development projects and other auxiliary uses. It has been an integral part of WFP's operations since its inception.

There has been concern that monetization may dilute efforts to reach the poorest and most vulnerable. The appropriateness of the beneficiaries selected for receiving Food Aid (q.v.) has also been called into question when the final resource transfer has not been in the form of food. Other monetization issues include the potentially negative effects of agricultural disincentives and market displacement, and the accountability, programming and management of the generated funds, although these concerns are normally related to the usually much larger flows of program food aid provided bilaterally.

Sales of WFP commodities are grouped in the following categories:

Category A: projects in which the sale of WFP commodities is an inherent part of the operation (e.g. dairy/livestock development, food reserves/price stabilization, and the manufacture of high-protein foods or livestock feed);

Category B: projects in which WFP rations are sold to closed groups of designated beneficiaries outside normal commercial markets;

Category C: projects in which part of the WFP commodities provided are sold on the open market in the recipient country.

In 1987, the Committee on Food Aid Policy and Programmes (CFA) (q.v.) endorsed a reference level of 15 percent for the sale of WFP commodities. The cumulative rate of monetization for the 1987–91 period was 13.7 percent. The majority of the funds generated were used to finance project activities although a significant proportion was used to meet WFP's ITSH (internal trade, storage, handling) subsidy commitments. Generated funds were also used to purchase non-food items for essential project support and to meet external overland transport costs.

CFA continues to monitor closely each session the monetization issue.

-N-

No entries

-O-

No entries

-P-

PERSONNEL. WFP has become a major provider of Food Aid (q.v.) in support of development projects, and the principal international channel for the provision of relief food aid. Within the UN system, WFP is now the largest source of grant assistance to developing countries, currently providing more than $1.5 billion of assistance annually to developing countries. With staff deployed in 85 countries, serving 92 developing countries, WFP has the largest global network for food aid. Its administrative expenses have been kept to less than six percent of annual expenditure. As of 1993, the personnel employed by WFP were, in general terms, classified as follows:

professional staff	470
support staff	1080
temporary staff	<u>1271</u>
total	2821

Approximately three-fourths of this total are assigned to WFP Country Offices in developing countries.

PLEDGING TARGET FOR 1995–96. In April 1993, the WFP Executive Director (q.v.) recommended for approval by the Committee on Food Aid Policy and Programmes (CFA) (q.v.) a pledging target of $1.5 billion for the Programme's regular resources (not emergency operations) for the next biennium, 1995–96. This is the same level as the current one approved by CFA two years earlier. This pragmatic approach was in large part based on the following consideration: Food Aid (q.v.) for development purposes has increasingly to compete with food aid for emergencies and refugee and displaced persons feeding operations. Further, the target for the most recently completed biennium, 1991–92, was only 77 percent achieved.

The proposal was submitted to that CFA session in order to permit ECOSOC and the FAO Council (q.v.) to consider the Committee's recommendations in June 1993, for presentation to the United Nations General Assembly and the FAO Conference (q.v.). If agreed to, then a Pledging Conference for the 1995–96 biennium will be convened by the Secretary-General of the United Nations and the Director-General (q.v.) of FAO before the end of 1994. (CFA approved the recommendation in its May/June session of 1993.)

PROJECT CYCLE. The conventional project cycle has, in general, been as follows: identification—design—appraisal—legitimation (CFA [q.v.] approval)—implementation (a third-country responsibility)—monitoring (donor and third country)—evaluation (donor). During 1985, the architecture for a revised WFP project cycle was defined and a beginning made on its implementation. The main features of the new system include:

(1) a country framework for deciding Food Aid (q.v.) issues and to build a stronger link between policies and projects;
(2) two major gateways in the consideration of projects enabling both WFP senior management and United Nations and specialized agencies to participate in acceptance of a project into the WFP pipeline and in final appraisal;
(3) improved project design, including clear objectives, analysis of costs and benefits, identification of essential inputs and planned arrangements for reporting, monitoring and evaluation;
(4) new criteria for judging the role and effectiveness of food as a project resource; and
(5) sharper focus on key implementation issues, including physical distribution management, logistic costs, counterpart funds, and resource accountability.

-Q-

No entries

-R-

ROBINSON, THOMAS C. M. (1912–1992). An American, born in Alberta, Canada, Robinson served with the U.S. Department of Agriculture (USDA) from 1935–62. During his years with the USDA, he was an Economic Counsellor in Karachi, Pakistan, and an Agricultural

Attaché in Australia. Thereupon, he became Director of WFP's Division of Operations. After Francisco Aquino (q.v.) resigned as Executive Director (q.v.) in 1974, Robinson was appointed to that position "ad interim" for 13 months; then, for four months in 1977, he was the Executive Director, until Garson Vogel (q.v.) was appointed to that position.

-S-

SUB-COMMITTEE ON PROJECTS (SCP). WFP's governing body's methods of work remained largely unchanged from its inception in 1962 as the Inter-Governmental Committee (IGC) to its 25th session as the Committee on Food Aid Policies and Programmes (CFA) (q.v.) in June 1988. The Committee traditionally held two sessions a year during which policy issues were discussed at plenary meetings. Projects and project-related matters were considered by a Sub-Committee of the Whole (SCW), with participation by members as well as observers. SCW, after having considered the projects, recommended them to CFA for approval. Questions were raised by Committee members about this way of conducting their sessions, particularly with regard to the project approval process. Many members felt that discussions on projects needed to be focused on technical issues, efficient use of resources, and populations to be targeted.

In response to concerns expressed over time by CFA members, the Executive Director (q.v.) in 1987 set up an expert group of eight members or former members of CFA, acting in their personal capacities, to formulate recommendations aimed at improving the working methods of the Committee. The principal recommendation of the expert group was that a Sub-Committee on Projects should be set up on a trail basis for three years. Subsequently, this recommendation, among others, was approved by CFA. It would be composed of 28 members, 18 chosen by the developing countries, 10 by the industrial countries.

It was decided that SCP would meet twice a year immediately preceding the sessions of CFA, for approximately one week. SCP was established to separate the project approval process from policy discussions, thus improving project consideration and allowing CFA to focus wholly on policy issues. It would also reduce the burden of representation by member countries. It was expected that discussions in SCP would be more technical and would be facilitated by having a smaller number of participants than SCW.

The main topics to be dealt with by SCP would be:

(1) development projects and budget revisions for CFA approval;
(2) review of progress reports and evaluation reports;
(3) protracted refugee and displaced person projects and budget revisions for CFA approval;
(4) emergency operation; and
(5) discussion of general project-related issues.

The most important innovation of SCP has been WFP-funded participation by a National Expert from the recipient country. The expert is chosen in consultation with the recipient government and is normally a government official who has been responsible at an appropriately senior level for the preparation and formulation of the project or who will be involved at a senior level with implementation of the project.

SCP in its present form is demonstrably a more technical forum than its predecessor, SCW. Participants do display technical expertise in development issues, project management, and the role and use of food aid as a development resource. Most SCP members are able to contribute to the debate, in a particular project context of project viability, proper targeting, likely benefits, or whether commodity exchange, Monetization of Food Aid (q.v.) or the payment of ITSH subsidies are appropriate components of the WFP-assisted project under discussion.

-T-

TRIANGULAR TRANSACTIONS. A triangular transaction is one in which food is purchased in a developing country and is used as Food Aid (q.v.) in another. WFP has become the largest purchaser of foods and services in developing countries among UN agencies and a major supporter of South-South trade. Triangular transactions are efficient in that they speed up the delivery of agricultural products to the recipient developing country; of equal importance, the purchases enhance the developing country which, at least temporarily, finds itself in a surplus situation.

TYPES OF PROJECTS. As reported in WFP's *1992 Food Aid Review,* the main types of WFP development projects are classified as follows:

Agricultural production. Projects to increase agricultural production, including land development, forestry, land rehabilitation, rangeland management, dairy and fisheries development, accounted for $1.3 billion, or 45 percent, of ongoing WFP-assisted development activities in 1991. In these projects, Food Aid (q.v.) is typically used either as food-for-work to support labor-intensive agricultural activities or as an incentive to encourage participation by local people in project activities or compensate them for the time they invest in the project.

Rural infrastructure. A major problem in many rural areas is the lack of physical infrastructure, such as roads to transport goods to market, water systems for human or agricultural use, and community facilities such as schools, health-care centers, and social centers. Food aid helps construct these facilities through food-for-work schemes. In 1991, the value of ongoing projects in this sector amounted to $326 million, or 11 percent of WFP development activities.

Settlement projects. Land settlement projects, in which new lands are brought into production by small-holders and agricultural infrastructure, public amenities, and civil works are constructed, accounted for seven percent of WFP's ongoing development activities in 1991. Food assistance tides settlers over the initial period until the first harvest or until self-sufficiency in food production is reached.

Food reserves. Support to national food reserves, market restructuring, and price stabilization activities form a small but important part of WFP's development work. In the case of food reserves, the objective is to improve the country's capacity to cope with bad harvests or natural disasters by ensuring a secure stock of staple foods for distribution at such times. WFP support for food reserves is usually undertaken in collaboration with other food aid donors; WFP often acts as a catalyst for bilateral contributions to government reserves.

In market restructuring or price stabilization projects, food aid is made available to governments for distribution, usually sale, when food prices are high. The proceeds normally are to be used to purchase local products at guaranteed prices after harvest, in order to replenish the reserve. Such projects help prevent excessive price fluctuations of staple foods which, if unchecked, could discourage local production (through producer prices falling too low after harvest) or cause excessive hardship to poor consumers (because retail prices rise to high levels prior to harvest).

Vulnerable group development. WFP food aid is provided to encourage greater and more regular attendance of mothers and young children at health centers. The food either provides a dietary supplement or constitutes a transfer of income to poor households or individuals because the food is in addition to their existing income. In institutional feeding projects, food aid may constitute budgetary support, allowing a government to expand or improve social programs, while providing recipients with improved diets.

School-feeding projects. School feeding alleviates short-term hunger, improving children's learning ability. The food also acts as an incentive to encourage regular attendance and as a dietary or income supplement to the family (helping compensate for loss of the child's labor while attending school). Sometimes WFP food also saves money in government budgets, which can be used for additional investment in education. More than one-fifth of total WFP resources for ongoing development projects, some $654 million, support education.

The effectiveness of WFP food aid for health and education depends crucially on the recipient country's efforts to improve basic services in these areas. The commitment of governments and the seriousness of their efforts are major factors in determining whether to begin or continue WFP support for health and education programs.

-U-

No entries

-V-

VOGEL, GARSON W. (1918–1981). Vogel was a Canadian, educated at the University of Winnipeg, with a degree in history and economics, and later a degree in law. He served with the Canadian Army in World War II, and thereafter held several important positions in the public and private sectors of Canada's grain industry. In 1971, Vogel became Chief Commissioner of the Canadian Wheat Board. Then, in 1977, he became Executive Director (q.v.) of the World Food Programme. Upon his death, in 1981, B. de Azevedo Brito of Brazil, who had been serving as WFP's Deputy Executive Director, was appointed Executive Director "ad interim," a position he held until April 1982 when James C. Ingram (q.v.) became Executive Director.

-W-

No entries

-X-

No entries

-Y-

No entries

-Z-

No entries

C. International Fund for Agricultural Development (IFAD)

-A-

AGREEMENT ESTABLISHING THE INTERNATIONAL FUND FOR AGRICULTURAL DEVELOPMENT. This Agreement (the official version is 43 pages) is the basic governing document of IFAD. The terms of the Agreement define and designate the organization, membership, functions, decision-making, resources, voting procedures, relations with other UN organizations, and amending process of IFAD. The Agreement was adopted by the UN Conference on the Establishment of an International Fund for Agricultural Development on June 13, 1976, in Rome; it was opened for signature on December 20, 1976, in New York; and it entered into force on November 30, 1977.

The Agreement has been amended, although substantive changes have been few. For example, the term of office of the President (q.v.) is now four, instead of three, years.

AL-SUDEARY, ABDELMUSHIN M. (1936–). Al-Sudeary was born in Riyadh, Saudi Arabia, in 1936, received a Bachelor's degree in agronomy from Colorado State University and a Master's degree in agronomy from the University of Arizona. For some ten years he held important positions in the Ministry of Agriculture of Saudi Arabia, then, in 1972, he was appointed by that government as its ambassador to the world food agencies in Rome. While occupying that position he was elected for a one-year (1976) position as chairman of WFP's Committee on Food Aid Policies and Programmes (q.v.). That same year, Al-Sudeary was elected Chairman of the Preparatory Commission, which successfully negotiated the establishment of IFAD. In December 1977, he was unanimously elected as IFAD's first President (q.v.), was reelected for a three-year term in 1981, and in 1983 that term was extended for one year.

AL-SULTAN, FAWZI HAMAD (1944–   ). Al-Sultan, born in 1944, is a citizen of Kuwait. He attended Beirut and Yale universities and later built an impressive career in international finance. He was the Managing Director of the Bank of Kuwait and the Middle East, Director of Research at the Kuwait Fund for Arab Economic Development, and subsequent to the Gulf War was made Director of the Kuwait Emergency and Recovery Programme. Thereafter, Al-Sultan was appointed to the World Bank as Executive Director representing the Arab States.

He was nominated by Kuwait in 1992 to be the new President (q.v.) of IFAD. There were two other nominees for that position, but both subsequently withdrew, so Al-Sultan was chosen by acclamation at the meeting of IFAD's Governing Council (q.v.) in Rome in January 1993.

-B-

No entries

-C-

CO-FINANCING OF PROJECTS. IFAD has always endeavored to optimize its own lending by seeking additional resources through co-financing, multilateral and bilateral. Also, it should be noted that for all IFAD projects initiated during the 1978–91 period, 40 percent were funded by the developing countries where the projects have been located.

Financing of Total Project Costs, 1978–91

Recipients	40.3%
IFAD	27.5%
Multilateral financing	26.0%
Bilateral financing	5.7%
NGOs	0.5%

An important aspect of IFAD'S operations has been the evolution of the share of projects initiated by the Fund, rather than by some other international body or industrial country. This evolution has come full circle, from 100 percent initiation of projects in 1978 by other financial institutions to 100 percent Fund-initiated projects in 1991. (See Charts and Tables, IFAD 4.)

-D-

No entries

-E-

ECONOMIC ADVANCEMENT OF RURAL WOMEN. A unique summit meeting was held in Geneva, Switzerland, on the Economic Advancement of Rural Women in February 1992. The summit was attended by 64 wives of heads of state or government, under the high patronage of Her Majesty Queen Fabiola of Belgium, and led to the adoption of the Geneva Declaration for Rural Women. The Declaration was subsequently endorsed by the UN Economic and Social Council and, according to IFAD, it evoked an unprecedented media response, with over one thousand press articles covering the issues. The Geneva Declaration calls for strategies to enhance the well-being of rural women, including the establishment of a global standing committee to monitor programs and policies which aim at raising women's income, productivity, and self-sufficiency. IFAD followed up the Declaration in a number of ways. For example, a communications strategy was designed in favor of rural women in Latin America and the Caribbean. In addition, an International Steering Committee has been set up and National Committees are in the process of being formed.

EXECUTIVE BOARD. The Executive Board consists of 18 members and 17 alternates, elected at the annual session of the Governing Council (q.v.), one-third from each category of the Fund's membership. Executive Board Directors serve for three years. The Executive Board is responsible for the conduct of the general operations of IFAD and, in particular, for the approval of loans and grants for projects. The Board has three regular sessions a year but may meet as often as the business of the Fund may require. During 1992, 24 new projects were approved by the Executive Board, bringing the number of IFAD-funded projects to 337 in 96 developing countries with loans totaling over $3.8 billion.

During the same year, the Board gave its approval for three Technical Assistance Grants totaling $3.2 million.

Among the Executive Board's activities and actions

in recent years have been: a review of a number of operational matters, such as its strategy for the economic advancement of poor rural women; financial matters, such as a drawdown (a tranche) of member's contributions; a special session (January 1991) to consider whether to recommend to the Governing Council a second phase for the Special Programme for Africa (q.v.) (it did so recommend); and a review of possible changes in the organization and staff of IFAD's Secretariat (q.v.) and (possibly) recommendations to the Governing Council for such changes.

In its December 1992 session, the Board approved the submission to the Governing Council of IFAD's 1993 budget specified in the following manner. The amounts for the Budgets and Programme of Work are specified below for both the Regular Programme and Special Programme for Africa.

IFAD Budgets and Programme of Work-1993 (US$ thousands)

	Proposed Administrative Budgets Excluding Contingency	*Agreed Programme of Work for Loans and Grants*
IFAD	54,900	341,000
Special Programme for Africa	6,279	84,000
Total	**61,179**	**425,000**

-F-

FINANCING. World Food Conference (q.v.) Resolution XII stipulates that contributions to the Fund would be on ''a voluntary basis.'' Moreover, the Fund was, in large part, a brainchild of the OPEC countries. A quadrupling of oil prices in the early 1970s had made the oil-rich countries wealthy, but placed in jeopardy the economic advancement of the non-oil, low-income developing countries. Reluctantly, the OECD countries agreed to the establishment of IFAD, but (according to their version of the agreement) on a 50 percent OECD-50 percent OPEC ratio of contributions. According to the OPEC countries, a 60 percent OECD-40 percent OPEC ratio had been agreed to. After lengthy negotiations the initial contributions to the Fund were just over $1 billion, some 57 percent by OECD countries, 41 percent by OPEC, and about two percent by the Category III countries (i.e., the developing countries).

By the Agreement establishing IFAD, not more than 12 percent of the funding can be in the form of grants, while the highly concessional loans are repayable over 50 years, with a ten-year grace period, at an annual service charge of one percent. Intermediate and regular loans are subsidized but at lower years of repayment and higher rates of interest.

In sum, IFAD is so designed that its Fund has to be periodically replenished. And "replenishment politics" has become a byword throughout IFAD's short history.

The First Replenishment, which took over two years to negotiate (1980–82), was slightly over the total of the initial contribution (see Charts and Tables, IFAD 2). The Second Replenishment required about another two-year period (1983–85), and a compromise figure of $460 million was finally agreed to by January 1986. However, the OECD-OPEC countries did agree to the setting up of a fund, ostentatiously titled the Special Programme for Sub-Saharan Countries Affected by Drought and Desertification (mercifully, the acronym is SPA), for which voluntary contributions were to reach the goal of $300 million.

In June 1989, again after extensive and intensive negotiations, a Third Replenishment was agreed to in the amount of $523 million. The much lower figure of the second and third replenishments can be accounted for in large part by substantially lower oil prices and the Iran-Iraq War.

In 1992, the Governing Council (q.v.) adopted a resolution which established the consultations on the Fourth Replenishment of IFAD's financial resources, and stipulated that those consultations must be concluded by the 17th session of the Governing Council in January 1994. (See High-level Intergovernmental Committee; Charts and Tables, IFAD 2.).

-G-

GOVERNING COUNCIL. There are presently 150 member-states in IFAD. Each is eligible to be represented, with voting privilege, at the annual meeting of the Governing Council held in Rome. These 150 members are divided into: Category I (OECD, 22), Category II (OPEC, 12), Category III (others, meaning developing countries, 116). However, the Agreement Establishing the International Fund for Agricultural Development (q.v.) stipulates that "the total number of votes in the Governing Council shall be 1,800, distributed equally among categories I, II and III." And Schedule II of the Agreement specifies how these votes are to be distributed within each Category.

Accordingly, it could be correctly surmised that the distribution and casting of votes would be complicated. But there are two important realities: (1) the decisions made at a Governing council session are arrived at very largely by consensus; and (2) with a few exceptions, the

Governing Council delegates its powers to the Executive Board (q.v.).

An annual meeting of the Governing Council is not, however, merely a showcase affair or a public-relations event. It is a political meeting, a kind of ratifying session, in which many informal discussions in closed rooms and hotel corridors result in the necessary compromises, or it is determined that a consensus position is not yet possible.

-H-

HIGH-LEVEL INTERGOVERNMENTAL COMMITTEE (HLIC). At its 10th session, in December 1986, the Governing Council (q.v.) agreed to the establishment of a High-Level Intergovernmental Committee on IFAD's Future Financial Basis and Structure (usually referred to as ''The Committee'' or by the acronym, HLIC). In organization, The Committee is legally composed of a maximum of 12 members from each Category (I, II, III). Actually, it was decided that there would be a 12-person committee, four from each category. As the full title states, its main purpose is to search for ways by which IFAD could be periodically replenished without being involved in seemingly endless negotiations (see Financing). Thus far, The Committee has had several meetings and few successes.

During 1992, four sessions were held to consider whether the political climate was such that a Fourth Replenishment could be undertaken with a reasonable likelihood of success. An informed consultation of The Committee did take place at the 1992 meeting of the Governing Council, and apparently there was at least a sufficient consensus to undertake negotiations for a Fourth Replenishment.

The OECD countries continue to claim that contributions should be kept at the original ratio; the OPEC countries argue that the ratio should be reviewed (i.e., a lower percentage of OPEC); while the Category III countries seem agreeable to at least maintaining their percentage of contributions made to the Third Replenishment. (For that replenishment, Category I countries contributed 79 percent, Category II countries 14.4 percent, and Category III 6.6 percent.)

There is agreement that the total figure for the Fourth Replenishment ''should approach $600 million.''

-I-

IFAD/NGO EXTENDED COOPERATION PRO-GRAMME (ECP). NGOs (Non-Governmental Organizations) are privately financed, privately organized and operated, religious or welfare-based, of which there are literally hundreds of importance to all the Rome food agencies. Food, farming, and nutrition often constitute a significant portion of their activities, although their ideologies, interests, and involvements frequently extend much beyond those functions.

A close and fruitful collaboration has grown up over the years between IFAD and various Non-Governmental Organizations sharing similar concerns and objectives. The common goal is to promote self-sustaining development initiatives at the country level by mobilizing participation by beneficiaries. The benefits from this collaboration with NGOs have been twofold. On the one hand, NGOs have an intimate knowledge and experience of the environment, culture and living conditions of IFAD's target groups, which have proved valuable in project design in allowing the beneficiaries' needs to be appropriately reflected. On the other, given their affinity of approach, NGOs have been instrumental in safeguarding and reinforcing the elements of IFAD's special concerns. NGOs have helped in promoting people's participation through the establishment and strengthening of local grass-roots organizations, which in turn also involve women in the process. Other areas of NGO intervention have been in the creation of farm employment opportunities for the rural poor, distribution of credit and inputs, and extension and training. They have also been active in a variety of social development programs, covering basic literacy, child care, health, and nutrition.

-J-

JAZAIRY, INDRIS (1935–   ). Jazairy was born in 1936, in Algeria. He is an alumnus of the Ecole Nationale d'Administration in Paris, and received Master of Arts degrees in political science (Oxford) and public administration (Harvard). Since then he has held several positions within the Algerian Ministry of Foreign Affairs and as an adviser to the President of Algeria. Subsequently, Jazairy has been a member or head of Algeria's delegations to many international meetings, and, from 1979 to 1982, he was the Algerian Ambassador to the European Communities, as well as to Belgium and Luxembourg.

When Jazairy was elected IFAD President in November 1984, consensus had reached rock bottom. The unique funding arrangement between the OECD and OPEC countries had begun to unravel, so he was forced to spend much of his time in negotiating what are termed "replenishments." However, it has often been said that IFAD was lucky; Jazairy, like his predecessor

Al-Sudeary (q.v.), has been a man of dedication, integrity, and imagination. Reelected in 1988, he retired at the end of his second term.

-K-

No entries

-L-

LENDING POLICIES AND CRITERIA. A basic IFAD document—*Lending Policies and Criteria*—reflects the broad objectives laid down in the Agreement (q.v.). It was adopted by the Governing Council (q.v.) at its 2nd session in December 1978. Therein are elaborated IFAD's objectives (increasing food production and decreasing rural poverty), its lending criteria (both country and project criteria), the lending terms and conditions (local cost and recurrent cost financing), and requirements concerning project preparation, appraisal, and monitoring. At the Governing Council's injunction, these are to be interpreted and implemented ''with necessary flexibility.''

Stated explicitly in the document (article 39) is the following directive: ''The Fund will seek to ensure that its lending policies and criteria are applied uniformly and consistently over the project cycle. . . .'' Further, it is required that all the projects assisted by IFAD must have a definite monitoring and evaluation component as an integral part of the project. (See Project Cycle.)

-M-

No entries

-N-

NON-GOVERNMENTAL PROGRAMS. (See IFAD/NGO Extended Cooperation Programme.)

-O-

No entries

-P-

PRESIDENT. The Governing Council (q.v.) elects the President by a two-thirds majority for a renewable four-year term. The President also functions as the chairman of the Executive Board (q.v.). This board meets only in executive session so the role played by the President in its decision-making is uncertain, but evidence obtained from interviews leads to the conclusion that the Presidents' influence is paramount. Until now, IFAD has had only three Presidents; each has been a ranking official in an Arab Middle East government. The President is assisted, especially in carrying out IFAD's administrative functions, by a Vice President, who has thus far been a U.S. official, usually of its Agency for International Development.

PROJECT CYCLE. Since its beginning, IFAD has viewed itself as a unique institution with a special mission for improving the lives of the rural poor. Consequently, the Governing Council (q.v.) has mandated that IFAD's project cycle should be both abbreviated in process and effective in results. As stipulated in *Lending Policies and Criteria,* the project cycle is, namely: project identification, preparation, appraisal, supervision, monitoring, follow-up, and evaluation.

IFAD's project and programming activities rely heavily on assistance from cooperating institutions—e.g., the World Bank, UNDP, regional banks, other UN specialized agencies, and bilateral institutions—at various stages of its work. The Fund itself, on a selective basis, has taken the lead in identifying and appraising projects in collaboration with member-developing countries.

Once a project has been approved by the Executive Board (q.v.) and a loan agreement has been signed, the basic responsibility for its implementation rests with the borrowing country. IFAD has cooperating arrangements with ten international institutions whereby they undertake, on behalf of IFAD, the supervision and loan administration of IFAD's projects. The supervision of the projects is entrusted to the cooperating institution appointed by IFAD. Increasingly, however, in order to ensure that the benefits of the projects go to the target group as desired, IFAD has been called upon to play a more positive role in project supervision. Thus, IFAD staff and consultants increasingly are involved in supervision missions.

Relative to the monitoring and evaluation of project developments, IFAD has introduced several innovations, and these have attracted considerable interest on the part of other financial institutions. However, some observers have claimed that IFAD's monitoring and evaluation unit, although fundamentally sound in its approach, is handicapped by a shortage of staff which in turn slows down the effectiveness of project implementation.

PROJECTS (SELECTED). In 1992, the Executive Board (q.v.) approved 25 project loans. A brief description, by IFAD, of 11 of these projects follows:

Country/Project Name	Loan Amount (US$ millions)
China: Jilin Low-Lying Land Development Project. The project aims to assist 73,500 very poor farming households which are adversely affected by difficult natural conditions to establish a more stable productive and sustainable system of agricultural production.	27.60
Ecuador: Saraguro-Yacuambi Rural Development. The project was designed to promote regional self-sustained development by increasing agricultural production particularly among small farmers while maintaining local cultural traditions.	16.70
Egypt: Newlands Agricultural Services Project. The objective of this project is to assist smallholders and other poor settlers in Egypt's reclaimed Newlands to establish sustainable and profitable farming systems through measures aimed at optimizing water use and at providing them with technical support, extension, and credit services.	25.00
El Salvador: Rehabilitation and Development Project for War-torn Areas in the Department of Chalatenango. The project is to help restore the social and productive base of the northern central area of El Salvador, an area particularly affected by civil strife during the ten-year war.	12.98
Guinea: Smallholder Development Project in the Forest Region. The IFAD-initiated and exclusively financed project will aim to regenerate Guinea's formerly dense forest, reduced in recent decades to savannah-type formations due largely to land clearance for shifting agriculture.	14.10
Indonesia: South Sumatra Smallholder Tree Crops Development Project. The project aims at assisting former transmigrant farmers	19.93

settled on tidal swamp sites of the Musi Delta region to increase their food security. The provision of credit and the organization of farmers into self-help groups are the cornerstone of the project's approach.

Iran: Agricultural Extension and Women's   20.10
Development Project.
The project aims at supplementing the country's agricultural extension activities by targeting poor smallholders, particularly women, to receive extension services in order to increase agricultural production and thus improve their income and standards of living.

Mauritania: Maghama Improved Flood Recession   10.94
Farming Project.
The project supports the government's objective of achieving food security by the end of the century, by improving upon a long-practiced production system based on flood-recession farming.

Mexico: Rural Development Project for the Indigenous   25.00
Communities of the State of Puebla.
The objective of this project is to improve the living conditions and incomes of approximately 17,000 rural families living in 400 indigenous communities in four regions of the State of Puebla, one of Mexico's poorest states.

Pakistan: Mansehra Village Support Project.   14.54
The objective of this project is to raise the standard of living of IFAD's target group—smallholders, livestock owners, the landless, and poor rural women—in a sustainable and environmentally sound manner.

Syria: Southern Regional Agricultural Development
Project-Phase II.   18.00
Phase II is expected to build on the potential for increasing the land planted to crops or fruit trees in areas where rocks reduce the cultivable land available, thereby enabling small farmers to earn a livelihood from this activity.

-Q-

No entries

-R-

No entries

-S-

SECRETARIAT. The Agreement which establishes IFAD stipulates that the President (q.v.) ''shall organize the staff and shall appoint and dismiss members of the staff in accordance with regulations adopted by the Executive Board (q.v.).''

As of 1992, IFAD's staff totaled 239, of which 96 here classified as professionals and 143 as general service personnel. This is an almost unbelievably low number, and is a principal source of complaint by IFAD's staff. However, the OECD members (led by the United States at the 1974 World Food Conference [q.v.] and thereafter) have intentionally demanded that IFAD should be basically a project-instigation and project-evaluation international agency. Article 7 of the Agreement stipulates that, ''for the appraisal of projects and programmes presented to it for financing, the fund shall, as a general rule, use the services of international institutions. . . [and] the fund shall entrust the administration of loans, for the purposes of the disbursement of the proceeds of the loan and the supervision of the implementation of the project or programme concerned, to competent international institutions.''

However, IFAD also engages the services of consultants and other temporary staff which enables it to meet its operational needs while maintaining a minimum of regular staff. Moreover, there is a good-sized loophole in Section 7 which reads, ''as a general rule,'' a phrase which IFAD interprets quite liberally.

SPECIAL PROGRAMME FOR SUB-SAHARAN AFRI-CAN COUNTRIES (SPA) IFAD was the first international financial institution to respond in the mid-1980s to the socio-economic crisis in sub-Saharan Africa. In 1986, the Fund initiated the First Phase of SPA-1 with a goal of mobilizing at least $300 million for that special fund. These contributions came from 19 industrialized countries, five developing countries, and the European Community. Another $123 million was mobilized from 15 international, bilateral, and other cofinanciers. Under this first phase, IFAD loaned over $338 million to 30 projects in 22 sub-Saharan African countries. The program's aim was to provide special assistance to African countries that were experiencing severe economic difficulties because of the continuing and devastating drought.

The severe drought continued so, in May 1991, IFAD's Governing Council (q.v.) authorized the second phase—SPA-II. By the end of 1992, eight countries had pledged $110 million to continue the program. SPA-II will support the setting up of rural small-scale enterprises in order to create non-farm employment for the rural poor.

SPECIAL PROGRAMMING MISSIONS (SPMs). These missions are sent to member countries, upon their request, to undertake an in-depth study of rural poverty along with an analysis of the macro-economic and policy environments, physical and institutional con-straints, and delivery mechanisms. The missions offer policy advice, and in many cases assist the member government in formulating an investment strategy for the food and agricultural sector and in identifying specific projects within that country which may later enter the IFAD project pipeline. By the end of 1991, IFAD had sent 44 SPMs to member countries and regional groupings.

THE STATE OF WORLD RURAL POVERTY. Three years in preparation, IFAD's major study, *The State of World Rural Poverty,* was published by New York University Press, and officially released on November 23, 1992. Its purpose was to directly and effectively address what is perhaps the gravest issue of our times, i.e., the growing number of rural people living on or below the poverty line. It is estimated that this number exceeds one billion persons, close to 60 percent of whom are women. In Africa alone, the number of absolute poor increased, it is estimated, from more than 200 million in 1988 to close to 300 million in 1990, or well over 60 percent of the African rural population.

This study is the first comprehensive profile of rural poverty in the developing countries. It presents a detailed analysis of the complex factors that cause and perpetuate poverty, factors that function in varying degrees from region to region, from country to country, even from locale to locale.

Women produce at least half of the food consumed in the developing world, and it is the report's contention, well documented, that rural development cannot suc-ceed unless women are included as equal partners in the development process.

-T-

No entries

-U-

No entries

-V-

No entries

-W-

WOMEN IN DEVELOPMENT PROGRAMME (WID). This program was initiated in 1989 and financed by contributions from the governments of Canada, Norway, Switzerland, and the United States.

In order to plan more appropriately IFAD's financial and technical assistance in this program, an analysis of women's household and agricultural tasks has been requested for all IFAD projects. A database has been established: (1) to provide country data on women in development; and (2) to develop an internal tracking system to assist in the identification of women as both intended and actual beneficiaries. All of this is designed to enhance the Fund's specificity in dealing with one of its key target groups.

Under the program, emphasis has been given to the briefing of IFAD missions on WID issues and the recruitment of consultants to develop project components which involve women on an equitable basis.

More extensive mechanisms are being established which will involve national women's organizations, both governmental and non-governmental, in the design and implementation of IFAD-supported projects. During recent years, an increasing share of IFAD's designated beneficiaries has been women. This process will be further consolidated in the future through a combination of specifically designed components and projects exclusively focused on women.

Also the number of IFAD women consultants participating in field missions during 1990 increased to 22 percent of the total number of consultants from a figure of 15 percent during 1989.

-X-

No entries

-Y-

No entries

-Z-

No entries

D. World Food Council (WFC)

-A-

AD HOC COMMITTEE ON THE REVIEW OF THE WORLD FOOD COUNCIL. For several years there has been considerable criticism, official and unofficial, of the role and functioning of the World Food Council. In its report on the work of the 18th session, held in June 1992, it was agreed that ''the Council has fallen short of achieving the political leadership and co-ordination role expected from its founders at the 1974 World Food Conference'' (q.v.). Thereupon the delegates agreed to establish an Ad Hoc Committee to develop and consider specific proposals for reorganization. All member states were invited to participate in this Ad Hoc Committee at a level of minister or delegate. By July 31, 1992, all proposals by member states for restructuring the Council had to be received by WFC's Executive Director (q.v.). Then, in mid-September, this Ad Hoc Committee met to consider these proposals and to report the results thereof to the UN General Assembly.

The principal conclusions of the Committee's report were as follows: In the view of several countries, the meeting of the Ad Hoc Committee only constituted the beginning of a consultative process on the options for the United Nations system and WFC for an enhanced response to food and hunger problems. They requested the WFC President (q.v.) and Vice Presidents to undertake intensive consultations with WFC member-states and the international community at large in preparation of the General Assembly's deliberations on the restructuring of UN activities in the economic and social fields.

ADVISORY GROUP. At the 11th annual session of the World Food Council in 1985, the delegates agreed that a review of the Council's jurisdiction was in order. The UN Secretary-General agreed and set up an Advisory Group of three persons, chaired by UN Assistant Secretary General Margaret Anstee. This Group submitted a report in February 1986 titled *Recommendations and Suggestions for the Future.* The report contained nine recommendations, primarily incremental in nature; i.e., do better what you have been doing with a small increase in financial resources.

At its 1986 session in Rome, the World Food Council took official notice of the Advisory Group's report, but the discussion was limited and inconclusive. Officially, it observed that there was a consensus that the Council was "playing a unique political role at the ministerial level and should continue to do so within its existing mandate." (See Ad Hoc Committee on the Review of the World Food Council.)

THE AFRICAN FOOD PROBLEM AND THE ROLE OF THE INTERNATIONAL AGENCIES. In 1980, the Lagos Plan of Action was adopted by the Organization of African Unity (OAU). Today that Plan is the most authoritative statement of the political will of African states to pursue "an effective agricultural revolution in Africa." The World Food Council endeavored to make a major contribution toward reaching that goal by holding a regional consultation in Nairobi, participated in by ministers of African states who were also members of the World Food Council. This regional consultation and the subsequent meeting of the World Food Council gave extensive consideration to the WFC Secretariat study, *The African Food Problem and the Role of International Agencies* (February 1982). This study concluded its presentation with the proposition that "the economic future of Africa is with the African farmer." This important truism was accompanied by a strategy, perhaps more a wish and a hope, whereby the World Food Council may assist in the fulfillment of this proposition by effectively coordinating the activities of some 30 international organizations which were involved in assisting developments in African agriculture.

-B-

BEIJING DECLARATION. This Declaration was unanimously approved by the member-states at the 1987 meeting in Beijing. However, the result was mostly rhetoric. It was acknowledged that "thirteen years after the World Food Conference . . . the number of undernourished men, women, and children in the world [had] risen," but the delegates were unable to agree on a specific and concrete course of action to alleviate that condition. This was a declaration of good intentions, weakly supported by statements which indicated a clear lack of political will to act. However, the Declaration concluded with the following statement: "We proclaim our intention to join together and, in our united strength and interest, to eliminate the scourge of hunger forever."

-C-

CAIRO DECLARATION. In 1988, Eduardo Pesqueira (q.v.), then President (q.v.) of the World Food Council, presented a report in Cyprus titled *Ending Hunger: The Cyprus Initiative.* At the World Food Council meeting in Cairo, in May 1989, the Council discussed the report and then adopted a set of conclusions and recommendations which formally became the Cairo Declaration. In the official summary, the report pronounced as follows:

(1) The world is now feeding more people than at the time of the World Food Conference (q.v.) in 1974. Despite this, hunger and malnutrition are growing and will continue to grow, unless nations— individually and collectively—take more efficient action in favor of the hungry poor.

(2) The biggest increase in the number of hungry people during the past 15 years occurred in Africa. Asia, however, still has the largest number of undernourished people—some 60 percent of the total.

(3) Most of the world's malnourished have neither land to grow enough food nor the income to purchase it, even when locally grown food is available.

(4) Hunger grows from the roots of underdevelopment and poverty. The rate of its growth reflects our failure to share this planet's food and resources in an equitable way within and between nations.

(5) This failure to share the world's food resources was most tragically demonstrated earlier in the present decade, when the growth in the number of hungry people accelerated, despite record-level global food stocks. Although these stocks have been sharply reduced recently, it is a fact of our times that hunger can no longer be blamed on inadequate global food supplies.

(6) The production of more food is essential to deal with current hunger and population growth, but

hunger will not be overcome unless the hungry have access to adequate employment or income-producing opportunities.

(7) Economic growth provides the means for making the elimination of hunger and malnutrition possible, but it requires policies and programs that direct its benefits to the poor.

(8) Countries that have truly made the elimination of hunger and malnutrition a key objective of their development have generally been able to make significant progress toward meeting that objective. These countries have often given higher priority to their food and agricultural sectors, made an explicit effort to employ their rapidly growing labor forces, and pursued judicious population policies.

(9) Ending hunger requires changes in current policies and the determination to end hunger forever.

(10) In order to eliminate hunger, it is necessary to improve the international economic environment, increase resource flows to the developing countries, and solve the problem of foreign debt.

(11) The World Food Council strongly believes that access to enough food should be proclaimed by the international community as a basic human right.

COUNCIL. The World Food Council is the highest political body in the UN system charged specifically with world food and agricultural matters. It has no operational functions, but is primarily an advisory, coordinating, and recommending body.

WFC has 36 member countries elected by the UN General Assembly for three-year terms—eight Asian, nine African, seven Latin American, eight West European, four East European, and the United States and

Canada. Twelve members of the World Food Council retire every year, to be replaced through elections by the General Assembly, on the basis of nominations by the Economic and Social Council. Retiring members are eligible for reelection; the United States has been on the Council since its beginning.

The Council is responsible for: (1) reviewing periodically, at the ministerial level, major problems and policy issues affecting the world food situation; and (2) making recommendations to the UN system, regional organizations, and governments on appropriate steps that might be taken toward the solution of world food problems.

CYPRUS INITIATIVE AGAINST HUNGER IN THE WORLD. The Cyprus Initiative, launched in 1988 at Nicosia, Cyprus, by Eduardo Pesqueira (q.v.), then President (q.v.) of the World Food Council, called for the combined efforts of member and non-member countries to eliminate world hunger and requested an action-oriented report. The final report, *The Cyprus Initiative Against Hunger in the World,* emphasized why certain policies had failed to halt growing hunger and endeavored to identify those which had been effective in ending hunger. It proposed a program of cooperative action which, at the national and regional level, would, if implemented, alleviate the severe problems of hunger and malnutrition which prevailed in most developing countries.

The report was presented to the ministers and plenipotentiaries of the World Food Council at its 15th ministerial meeting in Cairo, Egypt, in May 1989. They adopted a set of conclusions and recommendations to be known as the Cairo Declaration (q.v.).

-D-

DRAFTING COMMITTEE. The Council (q.v.) generally meets four times in open session at its annual meeting. The report of the drafting committee is acted on in closed session. A drafting group is appointed by the President (q.v.) to prepare the requisite set of conclusions and recommendations. The composition of this group is two representatives from each of the four regional groups (Asia, Latin America, Africa, Europe and Other States [this latter category including Canada and the United States]). The report of the drafting group will then be acted on by the Council, and almost certainly will be accepted by consensus.

Meetings of the drafting group—usually one long night session—are closed, but an observer may be given special permission by the President or the Executive Director (q.v.) to attend. And, at least on one occasion, this session will be characterized by lively, vigorous, and extended discussion; regional interests are defended, protected and (hopefully) fostered. The report is primarily an exercise in symbolic politics, but still meaningful.

-E-

EXECUTIVE DIRECTOR. This is the most influential position within the World Food Council. However, the Council (q.v.), although ostensibly the highest political body in the UN system in world food and agricultural matters, has no operational functions. It is primarily an advisory, coordinating, and recommending body. The Executive Director is an appointee of the UN Secretary-

General, which enables him to exert some political influence and leadership. But, his professional staff is small, only three professionals, with staff support of approximately the same number. Having neither operational nor financial functions, WFC has a very small budget (See Financing). After staff costs are met the Executive Director has very limited funds for research, consultations, policy coordination, or travel.

-F-

FINANCING. The World Food Council's relatively small budget is approved by and included within the budget of the UN Secretary-General, which is then submitted to the UN General Assembly for final approval. WFC's biennial appropriation for 1990–91 was nearly $6.4 million, and was increased to almost $7.3 million for 1992–93. However, the increase was due entirely to inflation and currency revaluations. This small budget has been of some concern to the WFC hierarchy and the Secretariat for several years. Nevertheless, since the Council has been constrained to depend on FAO for much of its data-gathering, research, and policy analysis, it has had difficulty in finding support for increased funding.

-G-

THE GLOBAL STATE OF HUNGER AND MALNUTRITION: [ANNUAL] REPORT. Each year since 1977 the Food and Agriculture Organization has submitted to the Council (q.v.) a report, usually titled *The Current World Food Situation.* In 1989, the WFC Secretariat presented to the Council a report on *World Hunger 15 Years After the World Food Conference: The Challenges Ahead.* Then, the next year (1990), the Council initiated its own annual report: *The Global State of Hunger and Malnutrition.* The 1992 "Global Hunger" report forecasts the various rates of economic growth in the developing countries, by geographic region. Very succinctly, the Council's forecasts for 1993 were as follows: per capita income in Africa will continue to decline; Latin America will recover from stagnation and contraction; East and South Asia will experience "robust growth."

-H-

HANNAH, JOHN ALFRED (1902–   ). Hannah was born in 1902, in Grand Rapids, Michigan, and educated at the University of Michigan and Michigan State University (B.S. and Doctor of Agriculture), and later awarded numerous honorary degrees. From 1944–69, he was president of his alma mater. Among his several important positions, national and international, Hannah was chairman of the U.S. Commission on Civil Rights from 1957–69, and Administrator of the U.S. Agency for International Development from 1969–73. He was Deputy Secretary-General at the 1974 World Food Conference (q.v.), and then selected in 1975 to be the first Executive Director (q.v.) of the World Food Council.

-I-

No entries

-J-

No entries

-K-

KALANTARI, ISSA. Prior to his election as President (q.v.) of the World Food Council in 1991, Kalantari was Minister of Agriculture in the government of the Islamic Republic of Iran. Officially, his term ended at the 1993 Council (q.v.) session. However, the Council did not meet that year. Its future status is still being determined by the United Nations.

-L-

No entries

-M-

MANILA COMMUNIQUÉ: A PROGRAMME OF ACTION TO ERADICATE HUNGER AND MALNUTRITION. This 1976 statement of resolutions came to be a kind of model for subsequent sessions of the World Food Council. In essence, the Communiqué constitutes a restatement of the principal resolutions which had been unanimously agreed at the 1974 World Food Conference (q.v.), plus a review of what had been done, or not done, to transform those goals or objectives into reality. The full text is some eight pages, but the main goals can be summarized, and the accomplishments evaluated, as follows:

(1) Increase food production—at least a four percent annual, sustained rate of growth in developing countries. This implied an estimated need of $8.3 billion a year in external financial resources (meaning from OECD countries). (Neither has been accomplished.)

(2) Improve world food security—achieve a new International Grains Agreement (which has yet to be done) and an International Emergency Food Reserve of 500,000 tons annually (which has been reached in recent years).

(3) Increase and improve the use of food aid (q.v.)—negotiate a Food Aid Convention (which was accomplished), and ensure a minimum annual level of ten million tons of cereal food aid (which has been achieved and exceeded in recent years).

(4) Improve human nutrition—a renewed emphasis on achieving this goal, by multilateral and bilateral agencies (in absolute terms, the worldwide numbers of malnourished is probably about what it was in 1974, but in that time world population has increased by over one billion persons).

(5) Improve the contribution of trade to the solution of food problems—negotiate an UNCTAD Integrated Programme for Commodities and renegotiate a new GATT agreement (the first was done, but not implemented; the GATT, Uruguay Round, negotiations are now in their seventh year of negotiation).

(6) Integrate these resolutions with other international development policies and programs—the main strategy was to persuade the UN General Assembly to enact a resolution committing each industrial nation to commit 0.7 percent of its GNP to official development assistance. (This has rarely been accomplished, except by the Nordic countries and the Netherlands.)

MAREI, SAYED AHMED (1913–1993). Marei was born in Egypt and educated at the Faculty of Agriculture, Cairo University. He farmed for a few years, worked for Egyptian agribusiness industries and soon became involved in Egyptian agricultural policy-making institutions. Marei was Minister of Agriculture and Agrarian Reform twice, assistant to the President of Egypt on two different occasions, and Secretary-General of the World Food Conference (q.v.), Rome, 1974. Marei served as the first President (q.v.) of the World Food Council, and was significantly involved in its origin and establishment.

-N-

NALLET, HENRI (1939–   ). Nallet was born in France and educated at the Institut d'Etudes Politique in Bordeaux. He was actively involved in French agricultural organizations and cooperatives, then served as Director of Research in the Department of Economics of the Institut National de Recherche Agronomique (INRA) for nine years, and later was agricultural advisor to the President of the Republic of France. He was elected a Socialist deputy in the National Assembly and Mayor of Tonnerre. Nallet was President (q.v.) of the World Food Council from 1985–87.

NATIONAL FOOD STRATEGIES. At its 5th (1979) ministerial session the Council (q.v.) recognized national food sector strategies ''as a promising instrument for food deficit countries to review their food efforts, to provide a framework for identification and preparation of investment projects and, where desirable, to step up the capacity and mobilization of investments, including additional external finance.'' Following the 5th session, some 30 countries, with a total population exceeding 400 million, indicated their intention to adopt a food strategy approach to the solution of their food problems, and most requested external assistance to support that undertaking. There was strong interest in a large number of developing countries in the food strategy concept and its use as a basic instrument to tackle domestic food problems as well as its utility to increase further the flow of development assistance to increase the production of food. At its 6th session the Council evaluated a report by its Secretariat on the experiences in the countries concerned, the effectiveness of the food strategy approach, and the support given it, as well as guidelines for its further application.

A major objective of the food strategy approach was to accelerate the mobilization of resources by providing a framework within which the so-called absorptive capacity problems might be overcome. Developing countries could thus clearly establish their preparedness to receive and utilize increased resources; developed countries and international agencies would then see clear scope for rapid and substantial increases in their assistance to food production. At least, this was the optimistic expectation.

The 1980 session of the World Food Council concentrated on the food strategy concept. Its common-sense quality was a major attraction. However, there have been two principal reasons for its limited success. First, the concept could only be successful, even in theory, if the industrial (OECD) members increased substantially their financial assistance to developing countries in the hopeful anticipation that it would be used to improve the overall food system of those countries. Their response was lukewarm and limited. Secondly, the food strategy concept was viewed with some skepticism by the developing countries—more specifically, the Group of 77. At the 1980 WFC meeting, the Group of 77 presented its "views and proposals" concerning the food strategy approach. In short, they contended that it could be viewed as a necessary strategy, but it would not be sufficient, and its adoption by a developing country should not be viewed as a precondition for additional development assistance.

-O-

No entries

-P-

PESQUEIRA, EDUARDO (1937–   ). Pesqueira was a citizen of Mexico, with university studies in law and economics. He served as director of investment and finance in the Mexican Ministry of Finance and Public Credit, representing Latin American countries on the World Bank Board, and was Director-General of the Banco Nacional de Credito Rural (of Mexico). He became Minister of Agriculture and Water Resources in the Mexican government in 1984, and was elected President (q.v.) of the World Food Council for the 1987–89 period.

PREPARATORY MEETING(S). Many of FAO's member-states have established a permanent delegation of some type (ambassador status or less) in Rome. It represents that member-state at the principal meetings of the Rome food agencies, either as a delegate or an observer. For WFC annual meetings the practice, until 1986, was for these Permanent Representatives to meet for a few days, usually in Rome, prior to the WFC meeting, to

discuss and analyze the papers which had been prepared by the Secretariat for that session, and then to
prepare a set of resolutions to be acted on by the
Council (q.v.). It was the intent of the Executive
Director (q.v.), and presumably of the President (q.v.)
of the Council and his cabinet, that these Preparatory
Meetings were only to discuss and make recommendations regarding those papers, and that the Executive
Director would thereafter draft a set of resolutions for
the Council to consider. However, these meetings were
usually dominated by developing countries because of
their sheer numbers and for some years the preparatory
sessions were much livelier sessions than the more
formal sessions of the Council. That is, the majority at
the Preparatory Meetings often desired and sometimes
endeavored to radicalize the Council agenda by making
recommendations, in the form of resolutions, of a much
more controversial nature with the hope and expectation that the forthcoming Council would react favor-
ably to those proposals.

In 1986, Executive Director Maurice Jacoultot Williams (q.v.) thwarted that strategy by simply abolishing
the Preparatory Meeting. That somewhat authoritarian
decision was apparently found acceptable to the President, Vice Presidents, and members of the Council. At
any rate, no Preparatory Meeting was held in 1986, and
none thereafter.

PRESIDENT AND BUREAU. Every two years the Council
(q.v.) elects a President and four Vice Presidents, one for
each region. The presidency is chosen, by informal
agreement, on a rotating basis by region. For a few years
the President was elected at the opening of the annual
Council meeting; then it was decided, in 1983, to elect
him, for the following two-term, at the conclusion of the
Council session in odd-numbered years so that the

President would have more opportunity to influence the policy proposals and actions of the Council. However, only President Arturo R. Tanco, Jr. (q.v.) has really provided dynamic leadership although it would be unfair to characterize the other Presidents as only chairmen of the three-day meeting, and it should be acknowledged that Tanco's accomplishments were decidedly limited.

The 1986 report of the Advisory Group (q.v.) did recommend that the Board (i.e., the President, Vice Presidents, Executive Director [q.v.], and Secretariat) should meet regularly each quarter, and that same Council acknowledged the wisdom of the proposal. Albeit, the Council's budget (funds appropriated by the UN General Assembly) were never sufficient to transform that recommendation into a reality (See Financing).

PROGRAMME OF CO-OPERATIVE ACTION. In 1989, the WFC Secretariat prepared a report titled *A Programme of Co-operative Action.* It called for cooperative action by Council (q.v.) members and the international community, and provided a set of proposals for concrete action as well as suggestions for overall policy directions and action guidelines.

The reaction at that Council session to this "Programme of Co-operative Action" was less than consensual. All the ministers welcomed the Programme, but the major food aid donors cautioned that it would be unrealistic to expect increases in Food Aid (q.v.) commitments, although it was agreed that efforts should be made to respond rapidly to food emergencies. Many of the developing countries favored the prepositioning of food stocks for emergency purposes, while the donor countries expressed concern that such a strategy would be difficult to implement in an efficient, cost-effective way. All this raised serious doubts about what could be expected and, in particular, realized in the way of "co-operative action."

PROGRESS TOWARD THE ERADICATION OF HUNGER: A MULTILATERAL DECADE FOR FOOD, 1974–1984. At their June 1982 meeting in Mexico, ministers at the World Food Council asked for a special assessment of the progress in meeting food objectives since the 1974 World Food Conference (q.v.), and the priority tasks which remained to be achieved. A panel of seven individuals with established credentials in the field of food and development from different regions of the world was appointed. They began their deliberations at a meeting in New York in March 1983 and completed them the following December in Rome.

The title of their report was *The World Food and Hunger Problem: Changing Perspectives and Possibilities, 1974–1984.* The conclusions of this study, considerably abbreviated, were as follows:

(1) Implicitly, a distinction was made between the world hunger problem and the world food problem, although the two are closely intertwined. While the production of more food is important to deal with hunger, especially at the local level and to meet population growth, hunger will not be ultimately overcome until the undernourished have access to meaningful employment and income-generating opportunities. These opportunities can come about, at least for the rural sector where most of the poor and undernourished live, only through greater output and productivity of the food and agricultural sectors. In the meantime, direct measures will be needed to provide the poor and undernourished with access to the food they require.

(2) The problem of hunger must therefore be tackled primarily at the national level. It is at this level that decisions are made not only about agricultural production and consumption, but also about the institutional structure of the economy, employment opportunities and distribution of income, management of money supply and credit, trade policy and exchange rates, all of which will have an important bearing on the overall food situation and the access of vulnerable groups to food. Both short-term and long-term policy decisions are required which provide for the immediate needs of the undernourished without hindering the long-term solutions to the problems of the food sector.

(3) The cause of the global food problem, as identified herein, has been the inability to reconcile the increasing commercialization of domestic and international agricultural trade with divergent national agricultural policies and expanding food surpluses. Without some measure of adjustment, the low-income countries will continue to face the relatively greatest brunt of this burden, affecting not only their food and agricultural sectors but the undernourished as well.

(4) To deal with the global food problem, changes in agricultural and trade policies in the industrially advanced countries are necessary, although it is recognized that given the production and income distortions that have already come about in the past, the process can only be gradual. The industrial countries should be in a much better position to deal with these internal reforms, for the domestic groups which may be negatively affected are rather small and the alternative resources to correct income effects to such groups are considerable. In the

present international situation most developing countries cannot define their agricultural policies without reference to international market conditions and prices. Developed countries must begin to shape national agricultural policies by understanding their implications on international prices and their impact on the low-income countries. This is the nexus where the global food and hunger problems come together.

-Q-

No entries

-R-

RABAGO, FRANCISCO MERINO (1918–   ). A citizen of Mexico, Rabago was an agronomist whose professional career began in 1938, when he became the first Director of the Banco Nacional de Credito Rural. He later became the Mexican Secretary of Agriculture and Water Resources, the post he held when he was elected President (q.v.) of the Council for 1981–83. Merino Rabago had also represented Mexico on IFAD's Governing Council (q.v.), and headed or was a member of his country's delegations at international meetings of FAO and the World Food Council.

THE ROLE OF TRANSNATIONAL CORPORATIONS IN FOOD AND AGRICULTURE. At the 11th session (1985) of the World Food Council, some delegates requested as a priority item the consideration at a future

Council session of the role of transnational corporations in the food sector. To assist in this study, the WFC Secretariat asked the UN Center on Transnational Corporations to cooperate. Jointly, the two prepared a "brief note" on the status of research on the role of transnational corporations in the food and agricultural sectors of developing countries. This study was released in March 1986: *The Status of Research Within UN Agencies on the Role of Transnational Corporations in Food and Agriculture.* This "brief note" (5 pages) is just that, but it does conclude that "transnational corporations are one of the major elements integrating the world economy. . . . " However, this important proposition has not been pursued further, at least not by the World Food Council.

-S-

No entries

-T-

TANCO, ARTURO R., JR. (1933–). A citizen of the Philippines, he was born in Manila, and educated in local schools and universities. He received further education in the United States at Union College, Cornell, and Harvard. Tanco was his country's Under-Secretary for Agriculture and Natural Resources, then Secretary of that department, from 1971–78. In that latter year (1978) he became a cabinet minister and a member of the Parliament. He was elected WFC's President (q.v.) in 1977, and reelected in 1979, serving until 1981.

TRANT, GERALD ION (1928–   ). Born in Toronto, Canada, Trant received his Bachelor's degree from Ontario Agricultural College and his M.S. and Ph.D degrees from Michigan State University. Later he served on the faculties of Ontario Agricultural College, Michigan State University, and University of Guelph. In 1975, Trant became an official in Agriculture Canada and later was appointed Senior Assistant Deputy Minister of that national ministry. In 1986, he was appointed to succeed Maurice Williams (q.v.) as WFC's Executive Director (q.v.). His term of office expired in 1992.

-U–

No entries

-V-

No entries

-W-

WALLY, YOUSSEF AMIN (1931–   ). A citizen of Egypt, Wally received his Ph.D in horticulture from Cairo University in 1958. He was a professor in the Department of Agriculture at Ain Shams University until 1982. Dr. Wally was serving as Deputy Prime Minister and Minister of Agriculture and Reclamation, as well as General Secretary of the National Democratic Party, when he was elected President (q.v.) of the World Food Council for the 1989–91 period. He was also scientific advisor to three National Ministries in Egypt, and was the editor of the Egyptian *Journal of Horticulture* for many years.

WHELAN, EUGENE F. (1924–). Born in Ontario, Canada, Whelan was educated in Windsor at a vocational and technical school, and became actively involved in Canadian farm organizations and cooperatives. He was a member of the Canadian House of Commons from 1962–85 and served twice as Minister of Agriculture. He was a representative of Canada to the World Food Council and, in 1983, was elected WFC President (q.v.), a post he held until 1985.

WILLIAMS, MAURICE JACOULTOT (1920–). Born in New Brunswick, Canada, Williams is widely recognized as an American international civil servant. He was educated at Northwestern University, University of Manchester (England), and University of Chicago. After four years of U.S. Army service in World War II, he became an economist and later a Foreign Service Officer in the Department of State. Subsequently he transferred to the U.S. Agency for International Development, where he became Deputy Administrator in 1970. From 1975–78, Williams was chairman of the OECD's Development Assistance Committee. Then, in 1978, he was appointed by the UN Secretary-General to be the Executive Director (q.v.) of the World Food Council. Since retiring from that position in 1986, he has been, and is, a senior research associate at the Overseas Development Council in Washington, D.C., as well as the Executive Secretary of the Society for International Development in Rome, Italy.

-X-

No entries

-Y-

No entries

-Z-

No entries

THE BIBLIOGRAPHY

INTRODUCTION

This bibliography has been organized as follows. First, there is a general section which cites books, monographs, and journal articles directly concerned with the four world food organizations. Most of these citations would probably be available in a major university research library. For a historical, institutional, and policy-making perspective of all these organizations the study by the author is instructive. The most comprehensive study of FAO is the book by Sergio Marchisio and Antonietta Di Blase, *The Food and Agriculture Organization.*

Then, each world food organization has a section which lists its major official publications. FAO has a far more extensive list of scientific, technical, and statistical publications than the others. For a complete catalog, interested persons should write to: Director, Publications Division, Food and Agriculture Organization, Via delle Terme di Caracalla, 00100 Rome, Italy. FAO's Rome headquarters would likely send a copy (at no charge), of its publication, *FAO Annual Review–1993* (latest edition). Ralph W. Phillips' indispensable study, *FAO: Its Origins, Formation and Evolution, 1945–1981,* was published in 1981 by FAO, and is probably available in major research libraries. Also, FAO publishes annually a study titled *The State of Food and Agriculture–1993* (latest edition), which would be useful to the interested lay person; it contains much statistical data. Finally, FAO publishes a bimonthly magazine called *CERES, The FAO Review.* Its journalistic type articles are usually about some policy or program concerning development, research, etc. in agriculture worldwide, and there is always a three-page section called "FAO in Review."

The World Food Programme publishes a quarterly *Journal,* which is aimed at general readers. WFP also issues annually an interesting and well-written volume titled *1993 Food Aid Review* (latest edition). Information as to their availability can be obtained from: World Food Programme, Publications Office, Via Cristoforo Colombo 426, 00145, Rome, Italy.

The International Fund for Agricultural Development publishes an interesting, data-filled annual volume, *Annual Report–1993* (latest edition). In recent years, IFAD has been issuing a brief, useful document titled *IFAD Update* (latest issue, No. 10, August 1993). Further information could probably be obtained by writing to: International Fund for Agricultural Development, Via del Serafico 1070, 00142 Rome, Italy. An IFAD study of major significance was printed for IFAD by New York University Press in 1992: *The State of World Poverty: An Inquiry into Its Causes and Consequences.*

Each of these organizations also has a Washington, D.C., or New York (United Nations) office, which may be able to furnish an interested person with instructive material.

Food and Agriculture Organization
Liaison Office for North America
1001 22nd Street, NW (Suite 300)
Washington, D.C. 20437

International Fund for Agricultural Development
Liaison Office
1889 F Street, NW
Washington, D.C., 20006

World Food Council
United Nations
1 UN Plaza
New York, NY 10017

World Food Programme
United Nations
1 UN Plaza
New York, NY 10017

1. GENERAL

Abbott, John. *Politics and Poverty: A Critique of the Food and Agriculture Organization of the United Nations.* London: Routledge, 1992.

Agresti, O. R. *David Sabin: A Study in Practical Idealism* [pre-FAO]. Berkeley: University of California Press, 1941.

Baker, R. J. S. "FAO and the World Food Situation: The Long and the Short Term," *The Political Quarterly,* vol. 50, no. 2 (1979), pp. 229–34.

Belshaw, H. "The Food and Agriculture Organization of the United Nations," *International Organization,* Vol. 1, No. 2 (1942), pp. 291–306.

Bolton, Brian. "Agribusiness and FAO: A Critical View," *Food Policy,* vol. 2, no.3, (1977), pp. 240–44.

Boyd Orr, [John] Lord. *As I Recall: The 1880s to the 1960s.* London: MacGibbon and Kee, 1966.

Cottam, Howard R. "The Role of FAO in Nutrition," in Jean Mayer (ed.), *World Nutrition: A U.S. View.* Washington, D.C.: Voice of America Forum Series, 1978, pp. 299–313.

Demongeot, Patrick, et. al. *World Food Program Assess-*

ment, Draft Final Report, plus Annexes I–III, Washington, D.C.: Office of International Development, Bureau of International Organization Affairs, Department of State, April 1986.

Dobbert, Jean Pierre. "Decision of International Organizations-Effectiveness in Member States: Some Aspects of the Law and Practice of FAO," in Stephen M. Schaubel (ed.), *The Effectiveness of International Organizations.* Dobbs Ferry, N.Y.: Oceana Publications, 1971, pp. 206–77.

Fauriol, Georges. *The Food and Agriculture Organization: A Flawed Strategy in the War Against Hunger.* Washington, D.C.: The Heritage Foundation, 1984.

George, Susan. "More Food, More Hunger," *Development: Seeds of Change* [FAO], Nos. 1/2 (1986), pp. 53–63.

Hambidge, G. *The Story of FAO.* New York: Van Nostrand, 1955.

Hobson, Asher. *The International Institute of Agriculture* [pre-FAO]. Berkeley: University of California Press, 1931.

Hopkins, Raymond F. "International Food Organizations and the United States: Drifting Leadership and Diverging Interests," in Margaret P. Karns and Karen A. Mingst (eds.), *The United States and Multilateral Institutions.* Boston: Unwin Hyman, 1990, pp. 177–204.

Horowitz, Irving Louis (ed.). "The UN's FAO: Is It DOA?", *Society,* vol. 25, no. 6 (1988), pp. 4–42. Articles by:
   1. Juliana Geran Pilan, "Becoming Part of the Problem," pp. 4–11.

2. Thomas D. Anderson, "Results Are Needed, Not Ideology," pp. 11–16.
3. John M. Cohen and Michael Westlake, "Advocacy Journalism and Development Policy," pp. 16–21.
4. Nicholas Eberstadt, "Official Evaluation and Agency Accountability," pp. 21–23.
5. Raymond F. Hopkins, "Shooting Yourself in the Foot," pp. 23–26.
6. Barbara Huddleston, "Why FAO?" pp. 26–32.
7. Richard Lydiker, "Setting the Record Straight," pp. 32–38.
8. Steven L. Varnis, "Policy and Performance in Ethiopia," pp. 38–44.

Hunt, Diana. "Policy 'Implementation': IFAD and Rural Poverty in Kenya," in: Clay E. J. and B. B. Schaffer (eds.), *Room For Manoeuvre: An Exploration of Public Policy Planning in Agricultural and Rural Development*. London: Heinemann Educational Books, 1984, pp. 101–26.

Jones, Joseph M. *The United Nations at Work: Developing Land, Forests, Oceans . . . and People* [a study of FAO]. Oxford: Pergamon Press, 1965.

King, John Andrews. "The International Fund for Agricultural Development: The First Six Years," *Development Policy Review,* vol. 3, no. 1 (1985) pp. 5–20.

Kriesberg, Martin. *International Organizations and Agricultural Development*. USDA, Foreign Agricultural Economics Report/31. Washington, D.C.: Department of Agriculture, November 1984.

Martin, William M. *Conference Diplomacy—A Case Study: The World Food Conference, Rome, 1974*. Washington, D.C.: Georgetown University, Institute for the Study of Diplomacy, 1978.

Marchisio, Sergio and Antonietta Di Blase. *The Food and Agriculture Organization (FAO).* Dordrecht, Holland: Martinus Nijhoff Publishers, 1991.

Matzke, Otto. ''Insufficient Control of Efficiency and Development in the U.S. System: The Example of the Food and Agriculture Organization of the United Nations (FAO),'' *Verfassing und Recht In Übersee,* 14. Jahrgang, 2. Quartal (1981), pp. 115–38.

Paulino, Leonardo A. and Shen Sheng Tseng. *A Comparative Study of FAO and USDA Data on Production, Area, and Trade of Major Food Staples,* Research Report 19. Washington, D.C.: International Food Policy Research Institute, October 1980.

Phillips, Ralph W. *The World Was My Barnyard.* Parsons, W. Va.: McLain Printing Co., 1984.

Riggs, Robert E. ''The FAO and the USDA: Implications for Functionalist Learning,'' *The Political Science Quarterly,* Vol. XXXIII, No. 3 (1980), pp. 314–30.

Schultz, C. F. ''UN Food Office [FAO] in Cairo Closed by Arab Pressure,'' *International Perspectives,* September/October 1980, pp. 22–25.

Sen, B. R. *Toward a Newer World.* Dublin: Tycooly International Publishing Ltd., 1982.

Shefrin, Frank. ''The Agriculture Agencies: Objectives and Performance,'' *International Journal,* vol. XXXV, no. 2 (1980), pp. 263–91.

Staats, Elmer B. *Staffing Requirements for the International Fund for Agricultural Development.* Washington, D.C.: Elmer Staats, February 1983.

Talbot, Ross B. *The Four World Food Agencies in Rome.* Ames: Iowa State University Press, 1990.

———. ''The Four World Food Agencies in Rome as Political Institutions: Toward 2000,'' *Transnational Law & Contemporary Problems,* vol. 1, no. 2 (1991), pp. 341–92.

———. ''The Four World Food Organizations: Influence of the Group of 77,'' *Food Policy,* vol. 7, no. 3 (1982), pp. 207–21.

———. ''The International Fund for Agricultural Development,'' *Political Science Quarterly,* vol. 95, no. 2 (1980), pp. 261–76.

———. ''The Role of World Food Organizations,'' in William P. Browne and Don F. Hadwiger (eds.), *World Food Policies: Toward Agricultural Interdependence,* Boulder, CO: Lynne Rienner Publishers, 1986, pp. 171–85.

———. ''The USA at the 9th World Food Council,'' *Food Policy,* vol. 10, no. 2 (1985), pp. 155–66.

Talbot, Ross B. and H. Wayne Moyer, ''Who Governs the Rome Food Agencies?,'' *Food Policy,* vol. 12, no. 4 (1987), pp. 349–64. Reprinted in: Birol A. Yesilada, et al. (eds.), *Agrarian Reform in Reverse: The Food Crisis in the Third World.* Boulder, CO: Westview Press, 1987, pp. 281–305.

Traylor, Julianne Cartwright. ''FAO and the Right to Food,'' in Asbjorn Eide, et al. (eds.), *Food as a Human Right.* Tokyo: United Nations University, 1984, pp. 187–213.

USAID. *Program Review of the International Fund for Agricultural Development.* AID Evaluation Special Study No. 21, Washington, D.C.: AID, January 1985.

U.S. General Accounting Office. *Status Report on U.S. Participation in the International Fund for Agricultural Development,* ID–81–83. Washington, D.C.: GAO, March 1981.

U.S. General Accounting Office. *The United States Should Play a Greater Role in the Food and Agriculture Organization of the United Nations,* ID–77–13. Washington, D.C.: GAO, May 1977.

United States Senate, Select Committee on Nutrition and Human Needs. *Hearings: U.S. Participation in the Food and Agriculture Organization of the United Nations,* March 4–5, 1976. Washington, D.C.: Government Printing Office, 1976.

United States Senate, Select Committee on Nutrition and Human Needs. *Staff Report: The United States, FAO and World Food Politics: U.S. Relations with an International Organization.* Washington, D.C.: Government Printing Office, June 1976.

Wallerstein, Mitchel B. and James E. Austin. ''The World Food Council after Three Years: Global Food System Manager?,'' *Food Policy,* vol. 3, no. 3 (1978), pp. 191–201.

Weiss, Thomas G. and Robert S. Jordan. *The World Food Conference and Global Problem Solving.* New York: Praeger Publishers, 1976.

Williams, Maurice J. ''Towards a Food 'Strategy for Africa,' '' [WFC] *Africa Report,* no. 28 (1983), pp. 22–6.

II. Official Documents

A. FOOD AND AGRICULTURE ORGANIZATION

Collins, Peter, et al. *Millions Still Go Hungry.* Rome: FAO, 1957.

FAO. *Basic Texts of the Food and Agriculture Organization of the United Nations,* Volumes I–II, 1992 edition. Rome: FAO, 1993.

FAO. *Commodity Review and Outlook 1993–94.* Rome: FAO, 1994 (latest edition).

FAO. *European Agriculture: Policy Issues and Options to 2000: An FAO Study.* London and New York: Bellhaven Press, 1990.

FAO. *FAO: The First 40 Years, 1945–1985.* Rome: FAO, 1985.

FAO. *FAO Fertilizer Yearbook: Volume 40, 1990.* Rome: FAO, 1991 (latest edition).

FAO. *Medium-Term Plan 1994–99.* Rome: FAO, 1993. (latest edition).

FAO. *FAO Production Yearbook: Volume 46, 1992.* Rome: FAO, 1991. (latest edition).

FAO. *Programme Evaluation Report 1992–93.* Rome: FAO, 1993. (Replaces the biennial Regular and Field Programme Reports.)

FAO. *Programme of Work and Budget for 1994–95.* Rome: FAO, 1993. (latest edition).

FAO. *Report of the Council of FAO,* 105th Session, 11–26 November 1993. Rome: FAO, 1994. (latest edition).

FAO. *Report of the First Special Joint Session of the Programme and Finance Committees on the Review of FAO.* Rome: FAO, May 1988.

FAO. *FAO Trade Yearbook: Volume 44. 1990.* Rome: FAO, 1991. (latest edition).

FAO. *The State of Food and Agriculture 1993.* Rome: FAO, 1993. (latest edition).

FAO. *World Agriculture: Toward 2000: An FAO Study.* New York: New York University Press, 1988.

Phillips, Ralph W. *FAO: Its Origins, Formation and Evaluation,* Rome: FAO, 1981.

Yates, P. L. *So Bold an Aim.* Rome: FAO, 1955.

B. WORLD FOOD PROGRAMME

WFP. *Annual Report of the Executive Director.* Rome: WFP, 1993. (latest edition).

WFP. *1992 Food Aid Review,* Rome: WFP, 1993. (latest edition).

WFP. *Food Works: Twenty Years of Food Aid for Development,* 1963–1983. Rome: WFP, 1983.

WFP. *General Regulations For the World Food Programme.* Rome: WFP, February 1992.

WFP. *Journal* (published quarterly). Rome: WFP, October-December 1993. (latest edition).

WFP. *Occasional Papers.* Rome: WFP, no. 1, August 1985. (E. J. Clay, *Review of Food Aid Policy Changes Since 1978.*) (No set schedule of publication, several others have been published.)

WFP. *Report of the Committee on Food Aid Policies and Programmes.* Rome: WFP, 1993, for the 35th Session, May 31–June 4, 1993. (latest edition).

WFP. *Report of the World Food Programme: Seminar on Food Aid.* The Hague: WFP, supported by The Netherlands Government, 1983.

WFP. *Ten Years of World Food Programme Development Aid: 1963–72.* Rome: WFP, 1973.

World Bank and the World Food Programme. *Food Aid in Africa: An Agenda for the 1990s.* Washington, D.C., and Rome: IBRD & WFP, 1991.

C. INTERNATIONAL FUND FOR AGRICULTURAL DEVELOPMENT

Alamgir, Mohiuddin and Poonam Arora. *Providing Security For All.* New York: New York University Press, for IFAD, 1991.

IFAD. *Annual Report 1992.* Rome: IFAD, December 1993. (latest edition).

IFAD. *Governing Council-Seventeenth Session Report,* (Rome, January 21–23, 1994. Rome: IFAD, May 1994. (latest edition).

IFAD. *Lending Policies and Criteria,* Rev. 1. Rome: IFAD, December 1978.

IFAD. *The Poor Are Bankable: Rural Credit the IFAD Way.* Rome: IFAD, March 1987.

IFAD. *IFAD Update* (issued quarterly). Rome: No. 10 is dated December 1993.

Jazairy, Indriss, et. al., *The State of World Rural Poverty: An Inquiry into the Causes and Consequences.* New York: New York University Press, for IFAD, 1992.

United Nations. *Agreement Establishing the International Fund for Agricultural Development.* New York: UN, 1977.

D. WORLD FOOD COUNCIL

The Advisory Group. *The World Food Council: Recommendations and Suggestions for the Future.* Report to the WFC. Rome: WFC, 1986.

WFC. *The Impact of International Agricultural Trade and Related Policies on Food and Development.* Report by the Secretariat. Rome: WFC, April 4, 1987.

WFC. *The Mandate, Functions and Future Role of the World Food Council, and Addendum.* ''Ad referendum'' reports of the Ad Hoc Committee on the Review of the World Food Council, to the UN General Assembly, September 16 and September 18, 1992, respectively. Rome: WFC, 1992.

WFC. *Report of the World Food Council, on the Work of Its Eighteenth Session,* June 23–26, 1992. New York: UN General Assembly, September 1992. (latest edition).

WFC. *Review of the Role and Functions of the World Food Council.* Background Note by the Secretariat, original and addendum. Rome: WFC, September 8 & 10, 1992.

CHARTS AND TABLES

I. Food and Agriculture Organization (FAO)

   1. Policy-making Structure
   2. Administrative Organization
   3. Programme of Work and Budget, 1992–93
   4. Expenditures from Extra-Budgetary Resources
      (selected years)

II. World Food Programme (WFP)

   1. Organizational Chart
   2. Financial Resources, 1963–92
   3. Development Commitments, 1963–91
   4. Food Shipments for Refugees, 1988–92

III. International Fund for Agricultural Development
     (IFAD)

   1. Organization Chart
   2. Initial Resources and Replenishments
   3. IFAD Loans and Grants, 1978–91
   4. Financing of Project Costs, 1978–91

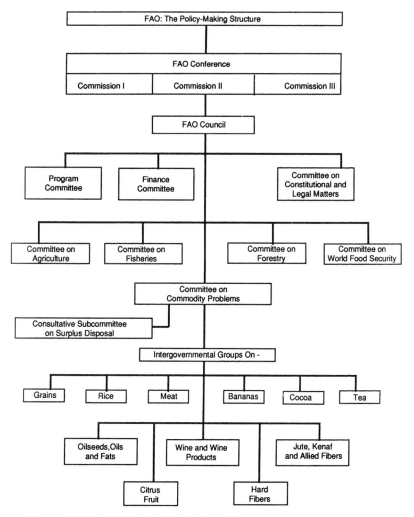

Source: USDA, *The Food and Agriculture Organization: Its Organization, Work, and U.S. Participation,* FAS M-2821, Washington, D.C.: USDA, June 1978, p. 7 (updated)

FAO ORGANIZATION

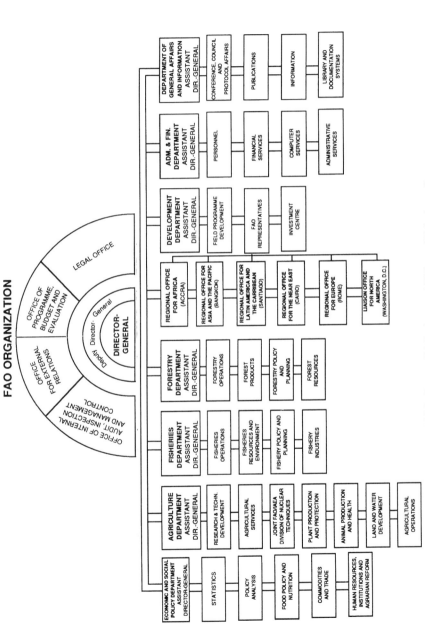

SOURCE: FAO, *FAO Annual Review* (1991). Rome: FAO, August 1992, pg. 23 (enlarged)

SUMMARY OF ESTIMATES BY CHAPTER AND MAJOR PROGRAMME
(US$ 000, all funds)

Major Programme/Programme	Regular Programme							Extra-Budgetary	Total 1992–93	
	1990–91 Budget		Programme Change	1992–93 Base	Cost Increase	1992–93 Budget				
	US$ 000	%				US$ 000	%		US$ 000	%
1. General Policy and Direction										
1.1 Governing Bodies	15 427	2.7	(408)	15 019	2 689	17 708	2.7	0	17 708	1.2
1.2 Policy, Direction and Planning	11 876	2.1	(455)	11 421	1 967	13 388	2.1	4 452	17 840	1.2
1.3 Legal	4 464	0.8	(10)	4 454	768	5 222	0.8	61	5 283	0.3
1.4 Liaison	10 327	1.8	552	10 879	2 046	12 925	2.0	1 219	14 144	0.9
Total Chapter 1	42 094	7.4	(321)	41 773	7 470	49 243	7.6	5 732	54 975	3.6
2. Technical and Economic Programmes										
2.1 Agriculture	212 643	37.4	(1 091)	211 552	31 495	243 047	37.3	564 901	807 948	52.7
2.2 Fisheries	36 399	6.4	(280)	36 119	5 691	41 810	6.4	66 689	108 499	7.1
2.3 Forestry	25 260	4.4	125	25 385	3 932	29 317	4.5	179 244	208 561	13.6
Total Chapter 2	274 302	48.2	(1 246)	273 056	41 118	314 174	48.2	810 834	1 125 008	73.4

			(9)							
3. Development Support Programmes										
3.1 Field Programme Liaison and Development	6 783	1.2	(9)	6 774	1 068	7 842	1.2	10 866	18 708	1.2
3.3 Investment	23 640	4.2	(736)	22 905	3 389	26 294	4.0	17 750	44 044	2.9
3.4 FAO Representatives	55 174	9.7	2 700	57 874	8 255	66 129	10.1	3 000	69 129	4.5
3.9 Programme Management	950	0.2	198	1 148	185	1 333	0.2	901	2 234	0.1
Total Chapter 3	86 547	15.2	2 154	88 701	12 897	101 598	15.6	32 517	134 115	8.8
4. Technical Cooperation Programme	67 767	11.9	4 000	71 767	5 642	77 409	11.9	0	77 409	5.1
5. Support Services										
5.1 Information and Documentation	22 122	3.9	(2 228)	19 894	3 419	23 313	3.6	6 095	29 408	1.9
5.2 Administration	55 080	9.7	(101)	54 979	10 737	65 716	10.1	22 058	87 774	5.7
5.9 Programme Management	2 452	0.4	(22)	2 430	447	2 877	0.4	572	3 449	0.2
Total Chapter 5	79 654	14.0	(2 351)	77 303	14 603	91 906	14.1	28 725	120 631	7.9
6. Common Services	17 836	3.1	(2 236)	15 600	1 178	16 778	2.6	2 255	19 033	1.2
7. Contingencies	600	0.1	0	600	0	600	0.1	0	600	1.2
GRAND TOTAL	568 800	100.0	0	568 800	82 908	651 768	100.0	880 063	1 531 771	100.0

Source: FAO, *Programme of Work an Budget for 1992–93*. Rome: FAO, July 1991, p. 63.

YEARLY EXPENDITURES ON FAO FIELD PROGRAMMES FUNDED FROM EXTRA-BUDGETARY RESOURCES
(US$ millions, by programme and programme category)

FIELD PROGRAMMES	1970	1975	1980	1985	1990	1991	1992*
1. FAO/UNDP Programme							
FAO execution	69.9	119.7	167.1	115.9	176.0	174.7	127.8
FAO implementation					5.6	5.6	8.3
Sub-total UNDP	69.9	119.7	167.1	115.9	181.6	180.3	136.1
2. Trust Fund Technical Assistance							
FAO/Government Programme	1.5	11.2	32.6	65.4	96.3	81.5	92.7
Assoc.Prof.Off. Programme	3.3	9.7	14.5	13.2	22.8	24.2	20.2
Near East Cooperative Programme	–	–	4.8	0.9	0.2	0.2	0.1
Unilateral Trust Funds	1.0	3.5	10.9	42.1	33.3	25.8	20.0
PFL Special Account	–	–	3.6	0.6	0.5	0.7	–
Freedom from Hunger Campaign/AD	2.3	2.7	1.6	1.1	2.6	1.1	1.1
UNFPA	–	1.9	3.5	2.1	5.3	9.1	3.3
UN Environment Programme	–	0.6	1.3	0.9	0.9	0.9	0.9
Other UN Organizations	1.5	0.4	1.7	9.4	7.4	6.8	6.6
Special Relief Operations (OSRO)	–	14.3	14.7	4.0	4.6	4.2	21.8
Int.Fertil.Supply Scheme (IFS)	–	53.8	3.3	1.5	0.3	0.1	0.1
Emergency Centre Locust Oper.(ECLO)	–	–	–	–	4.7	0.9	0.7
Screwworm Emergency Centre for North Africa (SECNA)					5.9	25.7	5.0
Miscellaneous Trust Funds	0.4	2.1	6.4	6.4	10.0	10.1	11.3
Sub-total Trust Funds	10.0	100.2	98.9	147.6	194.8	191.3	183.8
TOTAL EXTRA-BUDGETARY FIELD PROGRAMMES	79.9	219.9	266.0	263.5	376.4	371.6	319.9

* Provisional

Source: FAO, *Summary Programme of Work and Budget, 1994-95*. Rome: FAO, April 1993, p. 6.

WFP ORGANIZATIONAL CHART 1993

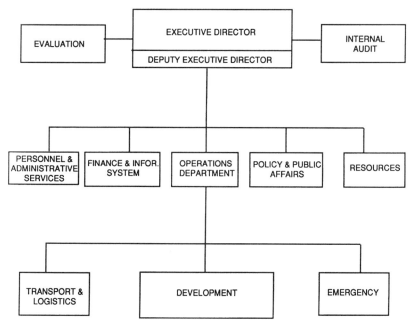

Source: WFP, *Annual Report of The Executive Director: 1992,* CFA: 35/P/h, April 12, 1993, p. 64

STATUS OF WFP RESOURCES FROM INCEPTION
(position at 31 December 1992)[1] (US$ millions)

Resources	Total	Commodities	Services and cash
Regular pledges:			
1st – 11th pledging period (1963–86)	6 344	4 800	1 544
12th pledging period (1987–88)	1 227	934	293
13th pledging period (1989–90)	1 203	905	298
14th pledging period (1991–92)	1 156	806	350
15th pledging period (1993–94)	436	292	144
Protracted refugee operations[2]	1 189	697	492
Food Aid Convention[2]	572	449	123
Directed donations	1	—	1
International Emergency Food Reserve[2]	2 691	1 777	914
Immediate Response Account	28	—	28
Government contribution (local operating costs)	15	—	15
Transfers from other funds	8	—	8
Net miscellaneous income	305	—	305
Support costs:			
Protracted refugee operations	5	—	5
International Emergency Food Reserve	7	—	7
Emergency logistic authorization replenishment	9	—	9
Total resources	15 196	10 660	4 536

Expenditure including unliquidated obligations against earmarkings already approved

Development and quick-action projects	8 824	7 091	1 733
Emergency operations:			
General resources	820	612	208
International Emergency Food Reserve	2 333	1 658	675
Immediate Response Account	13	—	13
Protracted refugee and displaced person operations	968	640	328
Programme support/administrative costs	859	—	859
Allocations:			
Insurance fund	13	—	13
Non-food items	11	—	11
Emergency logistic authorization withdrawal	10	—	10
Total expenditure	13 851	10 001	3 850
Net resources available for future commitments	1 345	659	686

[1]Provisional figures.
[2]Net of support costs.
Source: WFP, *Statistical Appendix to the Annual Report of the Executive Director-1992*, Rome: WFP, 14 April 1993, p. 5.

WFP DEVELOPMENT COMMITMENTS BY TYPE OF ACTIVITY, 1963–91 (US$ millions)

Year	Total	Agricultural and rural development										Human resource development						Other	
		Agricultural production		Rural Infrastructure		Settlement		Food reserves		Subtotal		MCH and primary schools		Secondary and higher educational training		Subtotal		Industry and mining	
		Value	%	Value	%	Value	%	Value	%	Value	%	Value	%	Value	%	Value	%	Value	%
1963–72	1 194	428	(36)	162	(14)	138	(11)	39	(3)	767	(64)	294	(25)	117	(10)	411	(35)	16	(1)
1973	129	52	(40)	27	(21)	7	(5)	-	-	86	(66)	28	(22)	15	(12)	43	(34)	-	-
1974	106	48	(45)	36	(34)	5	(5)	-	-	89	(84)	13	(13)	4	(3)	17	(16)	-	-
1975	393	133	(34)	41	(10)	46	(12)	-	-	220	(56)	169	(43)	4	(1)	173	(44)	-	-
1976	642	341	(53)	98	(15)	40	(7)	6	-	479	(75)	136	(21)	27	(4)	163	(25)	-	-
1977	367	125	(34)	35	(9)	56	(15)	-	-	222	(60)	125	(34)	20	(6)	145	(40)	1	(0)
1978	392	162	(41)	30	(8)	36	(9)	-	-	228	(58)	139	(36)	25	(6)	164	(42)	-	-
1979	492	217	(44)	62	(13)	44	(9)	4	(1)	327	(67)	149	(30)	16	(3)	165	(33)	-	-
1980	479	120	(25)	58	(12)	65	(13)	6	(1)	249	(52)	216	(45)	14	(3)	230	(48)	-	-
1981	543	202	(37)	105	(19)	128	(24)	14	(3)	449	(83)	75	(14)	19	(3)	94	(17)	-	-
1982	613	326	(53)	61	(10)	70	(11)	10	(2)	467	(76)	139	(23)	7	(1)	146	(24)	-	-
1983	696	343	(49)	63	(9)	66	(10)	-	-	472	(68)	208	(30)	15	(2)	223	(32)	-	-
1984	925	431	(47)	80	(9)	39	(4)	5	(0)	555	(60)	332	(36)	25	(3)	357	(39)	14	(1)
1985	642	345	(54)	102	(16)	37	(6)	15	(2)	499	(78)	107	(16)	37	(6)	144	(22)	-	-
1986	629	348	(55)	3	(5)	80	(13)	49	(8)	510	(81)	83	(13)	37	(6)	120	(19)	-	-
1987	621	211	(34)	70	(11)	17	(3)	-	-	298	(48)	307	(49)	16	(3)	323	(52)	-	-
1988	779	314	(40)	70	(9)	49	(6)	-	-	433	(56)	294	(38)	52	(7)	346	(44)	-	-
1989	575	326	(57)	21	(4)	39	(7)	1	(0)	368	(67)	162	(28)	26	(5)	188	(33)	-	-
1990	480	141	(29)	51	(11)	18	(4)	-	-	210	(44)	260	(54)	10	(2)	270	(56)	-	-
1991	448	189	(42)	92	(21)	5	(1)	6	(1)	292	(65)	134	(30)	2	(5)	156	(35)	-	-

Source: WFP, *17th Annual Report . . . to ECOSOC, FAO Council, and World Food Council*, Rome: WFP, April 1992, p. 26.

WFP SHIPMENTS[1] FOR PROTRACTED REFUGEE AND DISPLACED PERSON OPERATIONS, 1989–92 (thousands of tons)

Recipient	1989	1990	1991	1992[2]
Algeria	—	4.2	9.9	9.7
Costa Rica	—	1.8	—	—
Ethiopia	9.8	93.0	122.5	123.6
Honduras	—	5.6	—	—
Indonesia	—	1.0	0.9	1.0
Iran	—	30.3	72.5	51.7
Kenya	—	—	0.7	50.9
Liberia	—	—	24.0	111.1
Malawi	—	64.2	139.5	156.7
Mexico	—	2.5	4.4	4.7
Mozambique	0.1	45.2	83.8	120.1
Pakistan	20.0	193.2	384.8	287.4
Philippines	—	6.9	0.2	3.7
Senegal	—	4.8	11.7	2.3
Somalia	—	44.1	17.9	6.0
Sudan	—	19.5	35.6	55.6
Swaziland	—	0.5	0.2	0.6
Tanzania	—	0.1	—	0.1

WFP SHIPMENTS[1] FOR PROTRACTED REFUGEE AND DISPLACED PERSON OPERATIONS, 1989–92
(thousands of tons) (*Continued*)

Recipient	1989	1990	1991	1992[2]
Uganda	—	1.4	0.5	9.6
Zaire	—	3.6	0.7	8.8
Zambia	—	0.4	2.6	0.1
Zimbabwe	—	0.3	0.9	32.1
All recipients, of which:	29.9	522.5	913.2	1 036.0
Low-income, food-deficit countries	29.9	483.8	825.5	937.7
Least developed countries	9.9	264.0	427.2	591.8
Latin America and the Caribbean	—	9.8	4.4	4.7
North Africa and the Middle East		34.5	82.5	61.5
Sub-Saharan Africa	9.9	277.1	440.6	677.6
Asia and the Pacific	20.0	201.2	385.8	292.1

[1]Shipments based on bills of lading per year.
[2]Provisional figures.
Source: WFP, *Statistical Appendix to the Annual Report of the Executive Director—1992*, Rome: WFP, April 14, 1993, p. 35.

IFAD'S ORGANIZATION CHART (1992)

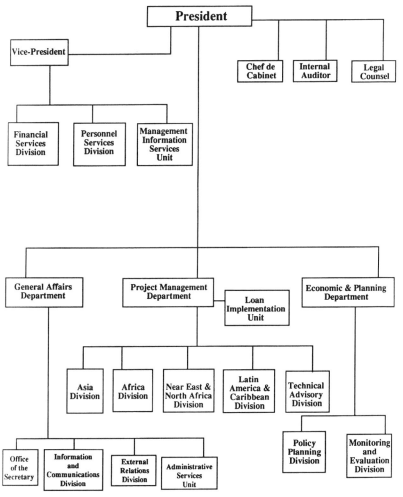

Source: IFAD, *Annual Report 1991*, Rome, December 1991, pp 24–25 (modified).

The Fourth Replenishment of IFAD's resources was the subject of wide discussions at the 16th session of the Governing Council on January 20–22, and at meetings of the three categories of member states held during the session.

The Council welcomed the report of the Chairman, Cheikh Abdoul Khadre Cissokho, Minister of Rural Development of Senegal, on the results of consultations on the Fourth Replenishment. These agreed that IFAD should continue to support poverty-alleviating projects in developing countries, with a main focus on promoting agricultural production and improving nutrition. The Council also agreed that, ''subject to agreement on fair and appropriate burden-sharing'' between the industrialized countries (Category I) and oil-exporting countries (Category II), US\$ 600 million ''would be an appropriate target for the Fourth Replenishment.''

The consultations must be concluded by the 17th session of the Governing Council in January 1994. For that purpose, the Executive Board may convene a special session of the Governing Council.

During the first round of consultations in Qatar last April, the Category I (OECD) countries stressed the importance of maintaining the burden-sharing arrangements, which are a traditional feature of IFAD.

The Fund was initially financed on the basis of Category I countries contributing 60% of funds and Category II countries, (the oil exporting developing countries) 40%. Category II countries stressed their belief that the ratio needs to be reviewed.

On average Category I countries have so far contributed 63% of IFAD's funds and Category II countries 34.2%. The remainder, 2.8%, has come from Category III (developing countries).

Under the third replenishment, which reached a level of US\$ 522.9 million, Category I countries have contributed

79%, Category II countries 14.4% and Category III countries 6.6% (as at the beginning of April, 1993).

Category III members say their contributions have been on a voluntary basis, by country, and cannot be considered as a level of pledge for the Fourth Replenishment.

The contributions of the three categories in the initial resources and three replenishments (excluding special resources for Africa) follows:

	(Expressed in US$ millions)	
Initial Resources:	**Total:**	**1000**
(Pledges of Member Countries)	Category I:	567
Effective 30 November 1977	Category II:	435
	Category III:	19
First Replenishment:	**Total:**	**1100**
Effective 18 June 1982	Category I:	620
	Category II:	450
	Category III:	32
Second Replenishment:	**Total:**	**488**
Effective 27 November 1986	Category I:	276
	Category II:	184
	Category III:	28
Third Replenishment:	**Total:**	**567**
Effective 24 December 1990	Category I:	378
	Category II:	124
	Category III:	65

Source: *IFAD Update,* Issue No. 8, April 1993, p. 3.

IFAD LOANS AND GRANTS UNDER THE REGULAR PROGRAMME AND THE SPECIAL PROGRAMME FOR AFRICA, 1978–1991 (US$ millions)

	1978	1979	1980	1981	1982	1983	1984	1985	1986	1987	1988	1989	1990	1991	1978–1991
Loans (US$ million)	93.4	326.0	332.6	306.5	284.8	259.8	189.1	120.2	138.3	211.6	229.6	259.9	307.6	275.5	3355.4
No. of Projects	8	21	27	30	25	24	24	16	20	24	23	23	26	22	313
Regular Programme (Amt.)	93.8	326.0	332.6	306.5	384.8	359.8	189.1	120.2	103.4	148.8	177.2	206.8	273.7	244.8	3086.6
No. of Projects	8	21	27	30	25	24	24	16	16	19	18	17	23	20	288
Special Programme (Amt.)	0.0	0.0	0.0	0.0	0.0	0.0	0.0	0.0	35.9	62.8	32.4	53.2	33.9	30.7	268.8
No. of Projects	0	0	0	0	0	0	0	0	4	5	5	6	3	2	25 1/
Grants (US$ million)	–0.0	5.5	13.1	21.5	16.8	17.3	13.3	10.7	8.1	14.3	13.0	12.5	15.0	5.5	166.4 2/
(No.)	.0	18	40	29	32	33	25	23	23	38	30	31	37	23	382 3/
Regular Programme (Amt.)	0.0	5.5	13.3	21.5	16.8	17.3	13.3	10.7	5.3	8.5	10.2	8.1	13.2	4.5	147.9 2/
(No.)	0	18	40	29	32	33	25	23	17	26	21	16	29	18	327 3/
Special Programme (Amt.)	0.0	0.0	0.0	0.0	0.0	0.0	0.0	0.0	2.8	5.8	2.8	4.4	1.8	1.0	18.5
(No.)	0	0	0	0	0	0	0	0	6	12	9	15	8	5	55
Total Loans and Grants (US$ million)	93.8	331.5	365.7	328.0	301.6	277.1	302.4	131.0	346.3	225.8	242.6	272.4	322.5	281.0	3521.8 2/

1/ Does not include four projects financed jointly under the Regular and the Special Programmes.
2/ This amount includes US$ 0.95 million under the NGO/HCP.
3/ This includes 15 grants financed under the NGO/HCP.
Source: IFAD, *Annual Report 1991*. Rome: IFAD, 1992, p. 64 (modified).

Financing of Total Project Costs
Regular Programme and Special Programme for Africa, 1978-1991

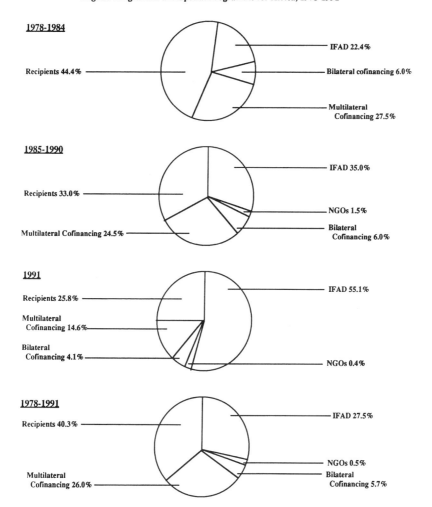

__1978-1984__

Recipients 44.4%

IFAD 22.4%

Bilateral cofinancing 6.0%

Multilateral
Cofinancing 27.5%

__1985-1990__

Recipients 33.0%

Multilateral Cofinancing 24.5%

IFAD 35.0%

NGOs 1.5%

Bilateral
Cofinancing 6.0%

__1991__

Recipients 25.8%

Multilateral
Cofinancing 14.6%

Bilateral
Cofinancing 4.1%

IFAD 55.1%

NGOs 0.4%

__1978-1991__

Recipients 40.3%

Multilateral
Cofinancing 26.0%

IFAD 27.5%

NGOs 0.5%

Bilateral
Cofinancing 5.7%

Source: IFAD, *Annual Report* 1991. Rome: IFAD, December 1992, p. 82.

ABOUT THE AUTHOR

Ross B. Talbot (A.B., Illinois Wesleyan University; M.A. and Ph.D, University of Chicago) is Professor Emeritus, Department of Political Science, Iowa State University, Ames, Iowa. For numerous years his research interests have concentrated on the politics of agricultural policies and programs in the United States, the European Community, and the international food agencies in Rome, Italy. In 1979–80, his sabbatical year was spent in Rome studying these agencies. Since then he has updated that research through their publications and through interviews and correspondence with officials of the U.S. Department of Agriculture, Department of State, relevant Congressional committees, and the FAO's and IFAD's regional offices in Washington, D.C. and with the office of the World Food Council, United Nations, New York City.

Among several other relevant publications, his study of these four world food organizations—*The Four World Food Agencies in Rome*—was published by the Iowa State University Press in 1990.